Chasing Rickshaws

Chasing Rickshaws

Published
October 1998

Published by
Lonely Planet Publications Pty Ltd A.C.N 005 607 983
192 Burwood Rd, Hawthorn, Victoria 3122, Australia

Lonely Planet Offices
Australia PO Box 617, Hawthorn, Victoria 3122
USA 150 Linden St, Oakland, CA 94607
UK 10a Spring Place, London NW5 3BH
France 71 bis rue du Cardinal-Lemoine, 75005 Paris

ISBN 0 86442 640 2

text & maps © Lonely Planet 1998
photos © Richard I'Anson 1998

Printed by The Bookmaker Pty Ltd
Printed in China

Chasing Rickshaws

Words Tony Wheeler   Richard I'Anson Photographs

Lonely Planet Publications   •   Melbourne   •   Oakland   •   London   •   Paris

Contents

Introduction

Born in Japan as the 'man-powered vehicle' or *jinrikisha,* the rickshaw later metamorphosed into the cycle-rickshaw and in parts of Asia is still the true developing world taxicab. Despite government opposition and competition for road space from faster motorized traffic, the cycle-rickshaw is still an enormously popular form of transport. Cycle-rickshaws are non-polluting, create employment at a relatively low cost and ideally fit the scale and traffic patterns of many Asian cities.

Also known as trishaws, sidecars, pedicabs, *cyclos, becaks* and a host of other local names, the cycle-rickshaw is much more than just a means of transport. The 12 Asian cities visited in this book cover the whole spectrum of the rickshaw and cycle-rickshaw story. In Beijing they disappeared during the Cultural Revolution only to reappear in the 1980s. In Penang the riders are old and fading, while in Manila they're often teenagers dreaming of moving on to jeepney driving. In Dhaka the cycle-rickshaws are both everyday transport and moving art galleries. In Singapore they're disappearing as day-to-day transport but simultaneously being reborn as tourist attractions. In Hong Kong they're both city icon and endangered species.

Not only does the rickshaw's position in the transport mix vary from city to city, the riders and other rickshaw people are an equally mixed bunch and they certainly have stories to tell. In our Asian travels we met with riders, owners, administrators, repairers, manufacturers and, of course, passengers. In Beijing we were lectured on how good rickshaw riding was for the health, in Calcutta we visited rickshaw pullers' dormitories and in Dhaka we talked to the artists who paint and decorate the region's most dramatically colorful rickshaws. In Hanoi we tracked down a scrapyard where confiscated rickshaws awaited their fate and in Penang we met up with the city official who put riders through their riding test. Our favorite passengers were, without doubt, the school children who, in city after city, pile into rickshaws to ride to and from school each day. In two cities, Beijing and Manila, we encountered women riders. Encouragingly, neither of them had experienced any difficulty breaking into an overwhelmingly male occupation.

The rickshaw designs are as widely variable as their riders. Hong Kong still has a handful of the old hand-pulled rickshaws and Calcutta is the only city on earth where they are still in use as everyday transport. In the other cities the rickshaw, a creation of the 1880s, gave birth to the cycle-rickshaw during the 1930s and 1940s but no standard pattern developed for this new-fangled device. In Manila, Rangoon and Singapore the cycle-rickshaws are standard bicycles with attached sidecars. The Manila versions with their mini-bikes and youthful riders look like a toytown model, while in Rangoon the passengers ride back-to-back. In Agra, Beijing, Dhaka and Macau the rider is out front and the passengers sit behind, as if the front part of a bicycle was mated with an old hand-pulled rickshaw. In Hanoi, Penang and Yogyakarta the meeting of bike and rickshaw produced precisely the opposite result, as if the back part of a bicycle had been joined to the old rickshaw seating; as a result the passengers sit, sometimes frighteningly, out front, watching oncoming traffic hurtling towards them.

Rickshaws have appeared in books and films – the becaks of Jakarta featured centrally in *The Year of Living Dangerously* while Calcutta's hard-working rickshaw wallahs were the stars of *The City of Joy.* The machines, their riders and their customers have been studied by engineers, evaluated by transport economists and analyzed by sociologists. They're celebrated in this book.

India's great icon, the Taj Mahal, defines Agra. Otherwise it's a just a middling-size city (population a little over a million) with a densely crowded *chowk*, or old quarter, and a sprawling cantonment dominated by an amazing number of military encampments. The imposing Agra Fort adds to the attractions but the horribly polluted Yamuna River is a definite detraction. Agra also has a huge fleet of rickshaws and the city's steady flow of international tourists keeps them very busy. Agra's rickshaw wallahs have a reputation for being a predatory band, happy to pedal tourists to the Taj but even happier if they can make a few detours to souvenir outlets and marble workshops on the way. Many of the city's rickshaw riders keep to the convoluted and narrow streets of the old quarter, but those who ply the tourist trade often have a good command of English and are happy to talk about the rickshaw business and their lives.

Rickshaw Design

Agra's rickshaw design follows the subcontinent norm, bolting the passenger seats and rear wheels on to a more-or-less regular bicycle front assembly. The rickshaws are smaller, narrower and much less colorful than their exuberantly gaudy Bangladeshi cousins.

Left
A softly spoken 65-year-old gentleman, Mohan came to Agra from Sukkur, which now lies in Pakistan, at Partition in 1948. He has been riding rickshaws for 40 years and has raised three daughters and a son; he told us that his son was 'doing well' as a car mechanic. Mohan rents his rickshaw for about 50 cents a day. Although he might only make a dollar on lean days, he typically collects $2 or more in fares. An occasional big day with foreign tourists brings in $3, supplemented by 5% commission from any shopping they might do.

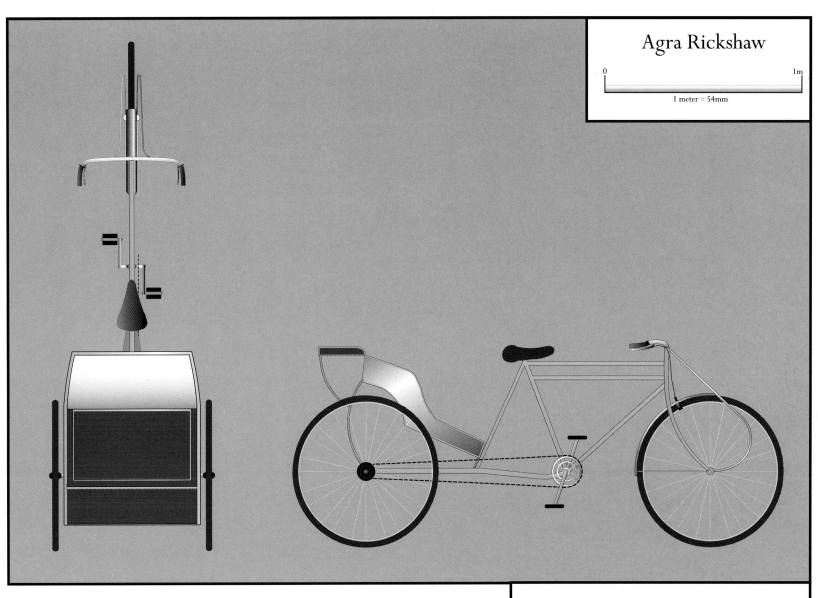

0   1m

1 meter = 54mm

number of rickshaws in city	5000	
weight	200 lbs	90 kg
wheelbase	71 inches	180 cm
overall length	99 inches	252 cm
track	31 inches	78 cm
overall width	32 inches	82 cm
passenger seat width	23 inches	58 cm
wheel diameter	28 inches	72 cm
tire size	28 x 1.5 inches	

Top left
Cycle-rickshaws regularly carry freight, like this load of metal containers, as well as passengers.

Left
Emblazoned across the back of Saleem Khan's rickshaw is the message: 'Gifted by Philip Freeborn, Cheshire, England'. Saleem had been a regular rider for the English visitor and his family when they visited Agra, and after they returned to England Philip Freeborn had sent the young rider the money to buy his own rickshaw. It's unusual for riders to own their own machine; most rent them out for under a dollar a day. The owner of a fleet might have 50 or 60 rickshaws, all rented out by the day.

Right
'Here I am,' a rider calls to a potential passenger in Agra.

Above
A rickshaw assembler bolts on the wheels.

Rickshaw Assembly

Left
Blue paint is applied to the frame of a new rickshaw.

Top right
Wheel hubs laced with spokes are ready to be built into new rickshaw wheels.

Bottom right
Narain Kumar Sawhney and his son Manish supervise rickshaw assembly at Sawhney Cycle Traders.

Sawhney Cycle Traders, run by Narain Kumar Sawhney with assistance from his 15-year-old son Manish, is a typical Agra rickshaw manufacturer. The dozen or so staff assemble, paint and finish up to 20 cycle-rickshaws a week. A brand-new rickshaw sells for less than $200.

School Delivery Service

Delivering children to school is a rickshaw activity in most of the cities we visited. For the rider, a regular school run is a guaranteed daily income – and although the fee per child is small, it's amazing how many children you can squeeze on to one rickshaw. Some rickshaws have clearly been fitted out with school deliveries in mind: a wooden plank across the front adds a whole extra row of passengers. Half a dozen older children is not an unusual load, and when it comes to tiny tots 10 or 12 climb aboard without a second thought. At the end of the school day in Agra, we would see the rickshaw-rider guardians carefully arranging each child on to his rickshaw, before hanging bags, lunch boxes (*tiffin* boxes as they're known in India) and thermos flasks off the vehicle's side.

Above
India is a crowded place so 10 neatly dressed school children is not an unusual load for an Agra school delivery rickshaw. School bags and thermos flasks hang from the handlebars and from each side of the rickshaw.

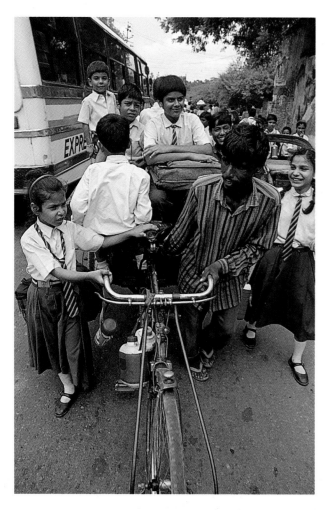

Above
It's not so bad once the rickshaw gets rolling but getting away from the rest with a heavy load of children is not easy.

Right
At the end of the school day it can be a complex process fitting all the children on board. The school uniforms are a clear reminder of the British influence on India.

Beijing

Left
Beijing's tricycles are less than elegant, especially with their ragged winter hoods. The Qianmen Gate at the southern end of Tiananmen Square is in the background.

The capital of China, Beijing is a sprawling city with a population of over 11 million and covers far too large an area to be served by cycle-rickshaws other than in small enclaves. Furthermore, *san lun che* (literally three-wheeled vehicles) were considered 'incorrect' by the Communists, and as a result started to disappear in the late 1950s. They were all but wiped out during the Cultural Revolution – some say they were completely eliminated but others insist that there were always a few tricycles around. They began to reappear around 1980 and now there is quite a thriving rickshaw population in Beijing. They are used occasionally by foreign tourists, rather more frequently by provincial Chinese visitors and even, to some extent, by Beijing-ites though they are more expensive than taxis. Possibly because tricycles have 'reappeared' after a period when they almost 'disappeared', most riders, even older ones, seem to be relatively new to the game.

Tricycle Design

Beijing's rickshaws have a surprisingly wide passenger seat, despite their relatively narrow width and extremely narrow track, because the smaller back wheels allow the seat to be mounted above rather than between them. As in Hanoi, braking is achieved by an external brake shoe working on a brake drum on the rear axle. The brake is operated by a long cable or length of bicycle chain reaching to the headstock, which is pushed by hand or foot. This crude braking system is kept in tension by a spring or by simply hanging a weight, often a brick or rock, from the back of the tricycle!

Left
Friendly Zhao Pei Tian has been pedaling around Beijing for 12 years. The board on the front of his tricycle advertises local hotels.

Top

Yao Yu Hai is 81 and has been riding rickshaws for 17 years, ever since quitting his factory job. Another rider told us that the younger riders all respected Yao Yu Hai and tried to push work his way.

Bottom

A bright and cheerful 62 year old, Yang Zeng Fui has been riding rickshaws for nine years. His children are embarrassed that their father rides a tricycle but he doesn't mind, he finds it an interesting and healthy occupation. He told us that none of his rider friends got sick and he himself had never been ill since he took up tricycle riding. A good day's work would net $10 or more. Everyone should make a contribution to society, he thought, and his was by riding his tricycle. He admired Princess Diana because she had contributed to society!

Above
Don't Like My Riding? Call the number on the back of the bike. All the tricycles have this phone number painted across the back.

Right
A flashy guy wearing a greatcoat, wreathed in cigarette smoke and with a jar of tea mounted on the front of his vehicle, Zheng Bao Zhong knows his tricycles and their politics. He's been riding rickshaws for 12 years. Pulling out a newspaper clipping from under his seat, he announced that the government had recently ruled that rickshaws were guaranteed an existence for at least the next 10 years.

Above
She wouldn't reveal her name but she told us she was in her 30s. She reckons she is the only female tricycle rider in Beijing. (In fact we only saw one other female rickshaw rider anywhere in Asia.) She gave up factory work to take up rickshaw riding a year previously. She owns her own rickshaw, enjoys the work, finds it lively, meets a lot of people and has no trouble being accepted by other riders – although some of her customers find it embarrassing to be pedaled around by a woman.

Left
Liu Sheng Jie in front of an antiques shop on Liulichang.

Top left
Tricycles waiting for tourists may have Beijing maps clipped to their handlebars.

Bottom left
Chinese bureaucracy in action – the top plate is the operator's driving license, the bottom plate is the business license and the blue medallion is the tax plate.

Right
Most Beijing rickshaws are fairly utilitarian but a few elaborate numbers congregate outside the Beijing Hotel, including this beautifully turned out tricycle, decorated with Tibetan art.

Ready for Winter

Unlike most cities we visited, nearly all the rickshaws in Beijing are individually owned (although it's said that at one time hotels had their own fleets and employed riders). Privately owned or not, the city's rickshaws all look rather rough and ready. This impression is not helped by their winter attire, which consists of either quilt-like curtaining (so it looks as if the tricycle has just been ridden through a bedroom and come away with the quilt draped over it) or flat sheets of plywood (so it looks as if the tricycle has just been involved in a collision with a garden shed).

Calcutta

Left
Rickshaws are often used for delivering goods as well as people.

Few cities on earth have a reputation as dark and desperate as Calcutta, with a large slice of its population of 12 million crowded shoulder to shoulder in crumbling colonial-era buildings or living hard-scrabble lives in the city's extensive *bustees,* or slums. Calcutta's hand-pulled rickshaws, most of them hauled by men from outside the city, immigrants escaping from even worse rural poverty, add to the air of despair. However, there's another Calcutta behind the facade, a city of art, literature and glimpses of almost magical beauty – whether it's flower sellers beside the Hooghly River or the stunning art produced for the annual Durga Puja festival and casually tossed into the river at the end of the festivities. Rickshaws are undeniably a part of the Calcutta experience. They're found congregating outside markets at dawn, carrying neatly uniformed children to school and even waiting to convey young couples home from the cinema in the evening.

Rickshaw Design

It seems obvious that the Calcutta rickshaw should have eventually evolved into the cycle-rickshaw but it could just as easily have evolved into a better hand-pulled model. In fact the rickshaws seen on Calcutta's streets in the last years of the 20th century are scarcely different from the original versions of a century ago. Some aspects of their design are actually inferior to the Japanese rickshaws of the 1880s and 1890s. Calcutta rickshaws still have wooden-spoked wheels and solid tires, rather than steel-spoked bicycle-type wheels and pneumatic tires. Cycle-rickshaws are found in the suburbs of Calcutta but they're banned from the city center.

Left
A Calcutta rickshaw wallah.

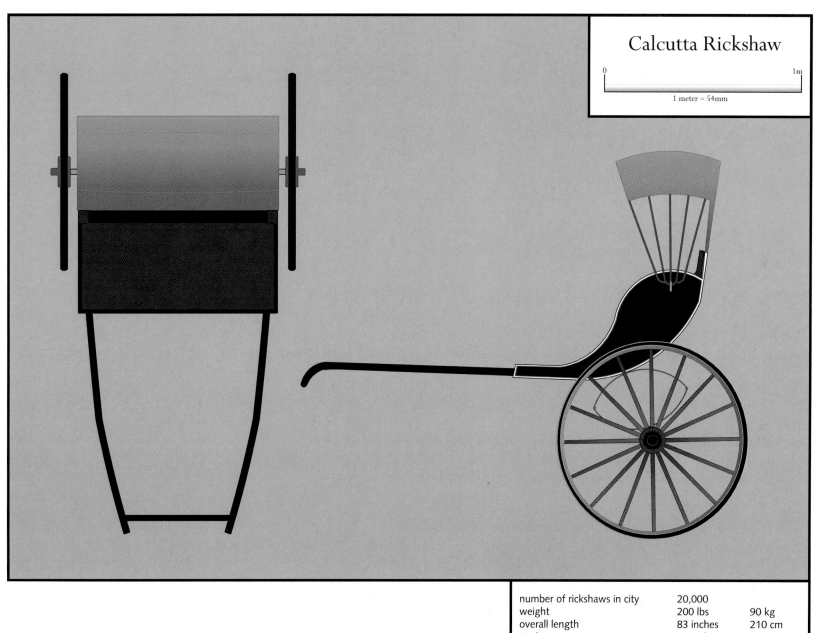

Calcutta Rickshaw

0   1m

1 meter = 54mm

number of rickshaws in city	20,000	
weight	200 lbs	90 kg
overall length	83 inches	210 cm
track	43 inches	110 cm
overall width	45 inches	115 cm
passenger seat width	26 inches	67 cm
wheel diameter	35 inches	90 cm

Rickshaws in Calcutta

Hand-pulled rickshaws still exist as tourist curiosities or historical oddities in very small numbers in several cities around the world. The historic city of Kurashiki in Japan has a few ready to be posed for photographs beside the city's picturesque canals and Hong Kong's final survivors, now down to single figures, hang around by the Star Ferry wharf on Hong Kong Island. Only in Calcutta in India are hand-pulled rickshaws still in everyday use as real transport.

Although Calcutta has the last remaining hand-pulled rickshaws it did not have the first, even in India. The first Indian rickshaws made their appearance in 1880 in the Himalayan hill station of Shimla, a hot season retreat for officials of the British Raj. This was the same year rickshaws were first seen in Singapore. It was a further 20 years before the first rickshaws appeared in Calcutta and then only for conveying goods. The first Calcutta rickshaws were not only owned by Chinese residents, they were pulled by Chinese immigrants. The Chinese workers have long disappeared but even today Calcutta's rickshaw pullers are mainly outsiders from the neighboring and even more poverty-stricken state of Bihar.

It was 1914 before rickshaws were finally allowed to carry passengers but through the 1920s and 1930s the city's rickshaw fleet expanded rapidly, even though by that time rickshaw numbers were declining in other cities. In 1939 the city authorities decreed an absolute maximum of 6000 licenses but after WW II the rickshaw population continued to grow. The combination of poverty, congestion and a ban on cycle-rickshaws in the city center encouraged the hand-pulled rickshaw numbers to reach 30 to 50,000 in the 1980s. In his bestselling novel, *The City of Joy*, Dominique Lapierre estimated that Calcutta's 100,000 rickshaw pullers handled one million passengers a day and covered a greater distance than the entire Indian Airways fleet of Boeing and Airbus aircraft.

Top left
Their last ride? A full load of chickens heads home from New Market, some of them suspended uncomfortably from the rear axle.

Middle left
In almost every rickshaw city there is steady business in delivering children to school. This neatly dressed group of schoolgirls look down disdainfully from their rickshaw on Roy St in central Calcutta.

Bottom left
It's early in the morning and two rickshaws provide the pause that refreshes for a weary rickshaw puller; he's probably been there all night.

Right
Rickshaws are often used for delivering goods as well as people but this hard-working rickshaw puller is doing both. Having loaded his purchases on to the rickshaw, the passenger climbs on top and heads home from the market.

In the Monsoon

Above
A hand emerging from a Calcutta rickshaw verifies the obvious – the monsoon is in full swing.

When the monsoon rains flood Calcutta's poorly drained streets the rickshaw truly comes into its own. Taxis may grind to a halt and who knows what's happening below ground, in the Calcutta subway system, but no matter how deep the water, the rickshaw will always get through.

Above
A plastic sheet protects the passenger but the rickshaw puller is out in the rain.

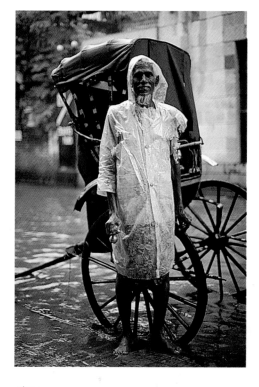

Above
A plastic raincoat keeps the monsoon rains at bay.

Left
Pulling a rickshaw in Calcutta isn't usually a cause for smiles but Abdul Adud manages one.

To Run a Rickshaw

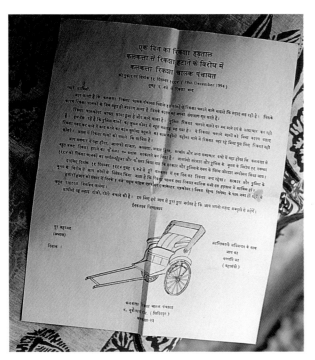

Anwar Hossain's rubber stamp proclaims that his business on Beniapukur Rd is a 'rickshaw garage', but actually it's far more. His 135 rickshaws come home to roost in the courtyard, but it also houses a busy little industry repairing and rebuilding older vehicles. Many of his rickshaw pullers also use the open building down one side of the courtyard as a crowded dormitory.

Anwar perches on a shelf at one end of the building, surveying his domain and keeping track of the paperwork which is an inevitable by-product of doing absolutely anything in India. Remarkably all the official forms and certificates for licensing, registering and operating a rickshaw in Calcutta are in English! There's an annual 10-rupee registration fee and six-monthly 15-rupee corporation road permits to be accounted for, adding up to about a dollar a year to keep a rickshaw legally on the road. The registration expiry date is stenciled on the back of each rickshaw. This paperwork is all stored in folders, along with letters and forms from the All Bengal Rickshaw Union and other important agencies, but the really important paperwork is a thick rectangular accounts book. In this a column of rickshaw numbers is followed by the names of the rickshaw wallahs who pulled that rickshaw on the morning shift and the afternoon shift. They're followed, of course, by the ticked columns which indicate the men have paid their 20-cent rental fees.

Right
Mohammed Khalid, a rickshaw puller at the Beniapukur Rd rickshaw garage, displays his 'Hackney Carriage Drivers License'. Renewing the license costs two rupees (about five cents) a year.

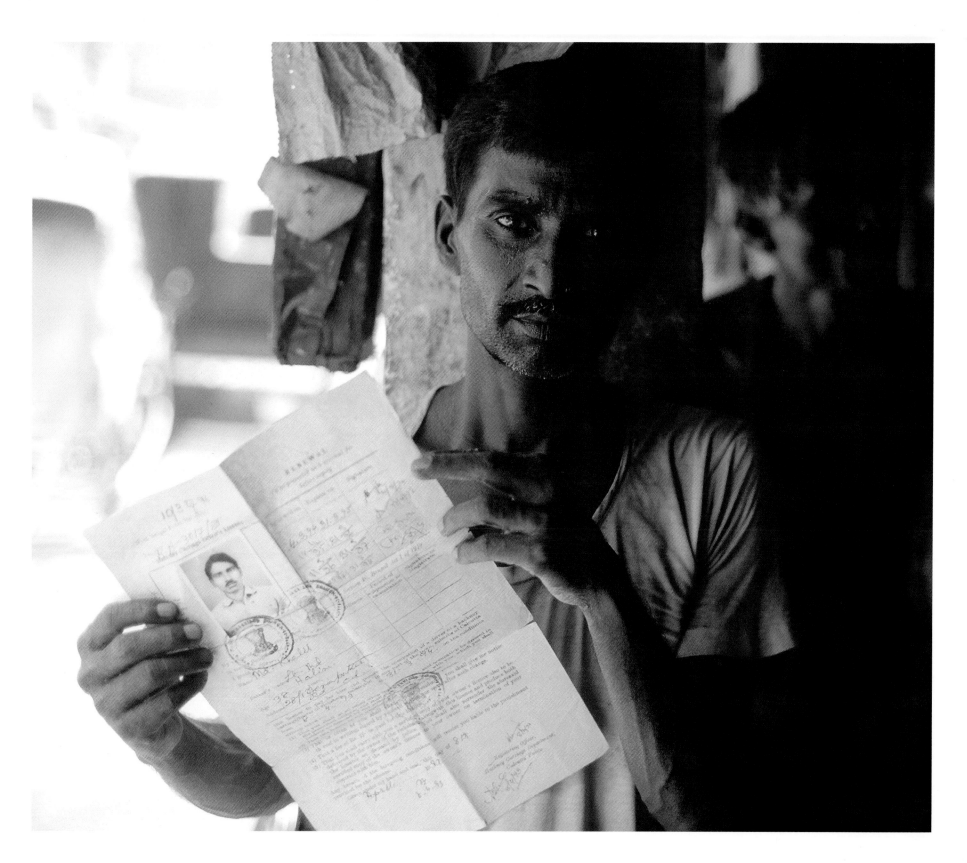

In the Dormitory

Calcutta's rickshaw pullers are often outsiders — temporary citizens of Calcutta, many of them from the impoverished state of Bihar. Rickshaw pullers often remit a considerable part of their income back to their families, whom they may only see once or twice a year. In Calcutta pullers often stay in large rickshaw dormitories, such as the one that runs down one side of the courtyard housing Anwar Hossain's bustling rickshaw business.

Top
The tinkle of a rickshaw puller's warning bell is one of Calcutta's familiar background noises.

Bottom
Anwar Hossain has a fleet of 135 rickshaws.

Left
The rickshaw pullers' dormitory in Anwar Hossain's depot.

Rickshaws & Politics

In late 1996 Subhas Chakravarty, the Transport Minister for the state of West Bengal and a member of the state's ruling Communist Party of India (Marxist) – it's typical of India that there should be two Communist parties, the CPI and the more successful CPI (M) – announced that the Calcutta rickshaw would be banned at the end of the year. When the city's 25,000-odd rickshaw pullers protested that putting a large part of the poorest people in the city out of work was a distinctly un-Communist thing to do, Chakravarty replied with the usual politician's platitudes, suggesting that jobless ex-rickshaw pullers could find work at truck depots around the city edge, if they ever got built. More tellingly he indicated that he really couldn't care less about the rickshaw pullers in any case, since most of them were non-voting out-of-towners. He announced that: 'We did not ask them to come here and do this.'

Naturally, India being India and Calcutta being even more Indian than the rest of that huge and often exasperating country, the plans to ban rickshaws soon got shoved on to the too hard pile and the city's rickshaws roll merrily on. Embarrassingly on, because if there is a job anywhere on earth which reeks of exploitation and indignity it must be pulling a Calcutta rickshaw.

The Workshop

In tiny Abdul Halim Lane a small courtyard shelters a hive of rickshaw activity. Indrajit Sharma's team of five restore and rebuild rickshaws, turning out a steady stream of shiny black 'new' vehicles. The seats may be covered in vinyl rather than leather but it's difficult to find any other components or techniques that weren't around 100 years ago. The huge 90-cm-diameter wheels are still assembled from 16 wooden spokes, slotted into a central wooden hub. A steel wheel rim clamps the solid rubber tire, which is cut in sections from old truck tires.

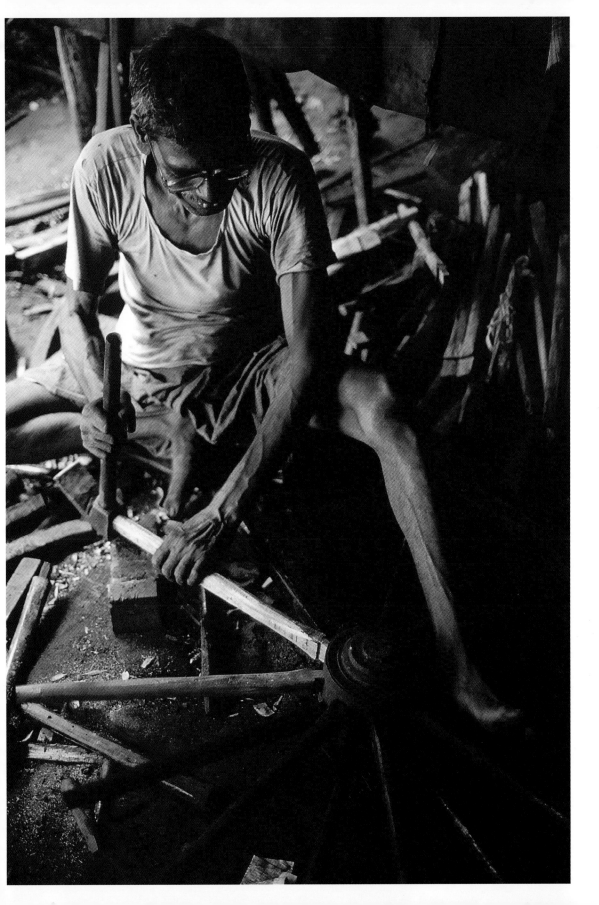

Left
Fitting new wooden spokes to a rickshaw wheel.

Top right
Fitting the axle to a rebuilt rickshaw.

Bottom right
The workshop owner Indrajit Sharma himself adds the red pinstriping, the final touch to a completely restored rickshaw.

Dhaka

Although Dhaka, with its population of eight million, is one of the world's largest cities, it only achieved capital city status with the division of Pakistan and the creation of Bangladesh in 1971. In no other country does the rickshaw play such a large part in the transportation picture – Dhaka is not only the capital of Bangladesh but also the world's cycle-rickshaw capital. It has been estimated that the city has over 300,000 cycle-rickshaws, many of them illegal and unregistered. Hardly surprisingly, this huge cycle-rickshaw population has a great influence on the city and many busy streets are almost awash with rickshaws, jammed in wheel to wheel in every direction. Yet at the same time there's remarkably little official recognition of the cycle-rickshaw's economic importance. The government's attitude almost seems to be that if they're ignored they might just go away and leave space for more modern forms of transport. Not only are Dhaka's rickshaws more prolific, they're also more colorful than anywhere else. Dhaka is where the cycle-rickshaw becomes a mobile work of art.

Backstreet Traffic

Major traffic junctions during the rush hour are not the only places in Dhaka where a glut of rickshaws can bring movement to a halt. In narrow back alleys, often barely wide enough for two rickshaws to pass, it only takes a minor mishap or the untimely arrival of a four-wheeled intruder for movement to grind to a halt. Within seconds a third, a fourth, a tenth, a twentieth rickshaw will join the melee and within minutes a string of stationary rickshaws will be lined up as far as the eye can see in both directions.

Left
A rickshaw rider peeps through the rear window of his extravagantly decorated machine.

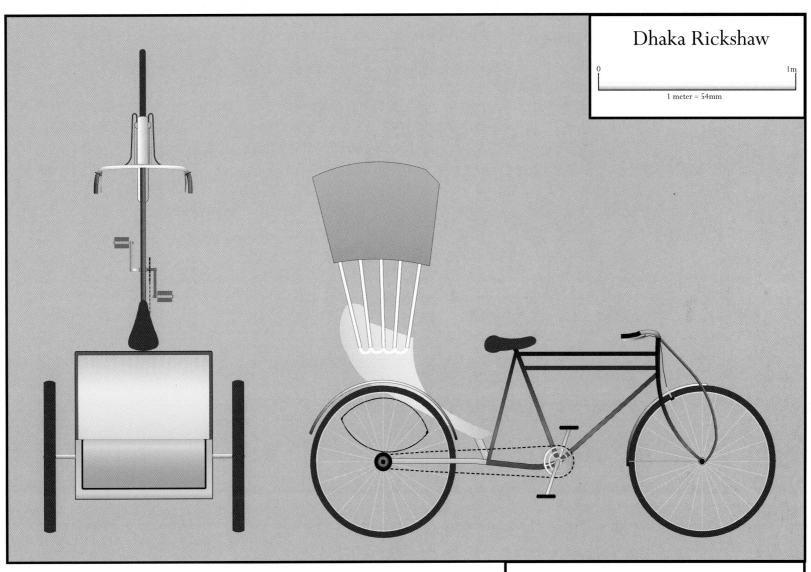

0   1m

1 meter = 54mm

Rickshaw Design

The Dhaka rickshaw follows the standard subcontinent design, linking an off-the-shelf bicycle front assembly with a rear subframe carrying the passenger seat and rear wheels. Because there are so many of them, the machines have been intensively studied by overseas aid schemes. They have concluded that the Dhaka rickshaw is overweight yet lacking in strength and reliability, poorly braked, unstable, difficult to steer and, because there are no gears, hard work to propel. Identifying the problems has been relatively easy; coming up with a new, improved rickshaw has been much less straight-forward.

number of rickshaws in city	300,000	
weight	200 lbs	90 kg
wheelbase	65 inches	166 cm
overall length	94 inches	238 cm
track	39 inches	100 cm
overall width	43 inches	110 cm
passenger seat width	24 inches	60 cm
wheel diameter	28 inches	72 cm
tire size	28 x 1.5 inches	

Heavy Traffic

The Grand Palace International Hotel in Dhaka is neither grand nor a palace and it's international only because Richard and I are staying there. From my room, however, I can see at a glance why this is the world's cycle-rickshaw capital. I'm poised directly over the junction of Fulbaria Rd and North-South Rd at Gulistan Crossing and traffic fights its way across what must be the busiest intersection in the city night and day. It's relatively calm in the early hours of the morning, apart from the occasional big bus whose driver can't resist blasting his horn every 100 meters no matter what the time is, but for much of the day the intersection is far from quiet and in the afternoon rush hour it's a gridlock scene which would surpass the worst night-mares of any Manhattan traffic controller. It's not cars, taxis or buses which are causing the snarl, it's rickshaws ... hundreds of them, thousands of them, packed in wheel to wheel, bells furiously clanging and all of them going nowhere.

Nobody really knows how many rickshaws there are in Dhaka. Officially there are around 100,000 registered and recorded in the city statistics, with three or four times as many in the whole country. Unofficially the number is far, far higher. Realistically there are probably a third of a million cycle-rickshaws in Dhaka alone.

Rickshaws utterly dominate local traffic. Sure there are some major routes where cycle-rickshaws are banned, but in comparison to the seething rickshaw masses, cars are few and far between, taxis are almost non-existent and even the auto-rickshaws, known locally as 'baby taxis', are a long way back in the population race. In Bangladesh's total expenditure on transport, rickshaws take the single biggest bite. It has been estimated that one taka in every three spent on transport goes to the rickshaw business, which is twice as big as Bangladesh Biman, the national airline.

Right
Rickshaws and baby taxis, the motor-scooter like vehicles known in India as auto-rickshaws, fight for space in central Dhaka.

Next page
With more than a third of a million rickshaws filling the streets of Dhaka, traffic jams like this one in Old Dhaka are commonplace.

Living with Rickshaws

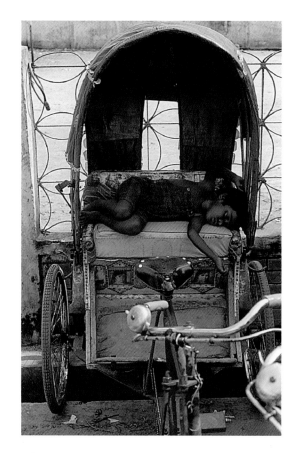

Left
A full load of passengers outside Sadarghat Market.

Above
A pint-sized rickshaw wallah takes a well-earned rickshaw rest.

Right
Outside of Dhaka much of low-lying Bangladesh seems to be under water for the greater part of the year. It's hardly surprising that, after rickshaws, the most popular form of transport is probably ferry boats. There's plenty of water to keep a rickshaw clean.

Mysteris, Maleks & Mastans

What do you do when your rickshaw gets a puncture, the chain breaks or a pedal falls off? You turn to the nearest *mysteri*. Mysteris are the mechanics, found wherever there are rickshaws, perched by the roadside with a boxful of tools, ready to work on rickshaw problems. Many mysteris also own rickshaws, which they rent out to rickshaw pullers. Rickshaw licenses are an equally tradeable commodity, rented out by mysteris to rickshaw owners who do not have the licenses to operate their vehicles. A well-established mysteri might own three or four rickshaws and a number of licenses.

Most rickshaw pullers can only dream of owning their rickshaw but a substantial minority, about 10% in Dhaka and even more in smaller cities, do own their vehicle. Some do so well that they manage to buy a second or even a third rickshaw. Maintaining three rickshaws leaves little time for riding one of them, so a rickshaw rider with three rickshaws would probably become a mysteri and make a living from renting his own rickshaws and servicing and repairing other riders' vehicles.

Top
Pushing a heavily laden rickshaw through the mud outside Sadarghat Market on the riverside Buckland Bund in Old Dhaka.

Bottom
North-South Rd near Gulistan Crossing is the most rickshaw saturated artery in the city.

In *The Rickshaws of Bangladesh*, Rob Gallagher's detailed study of the rickshaw business, the author traces the convoluted path from puller to mysteri to the really big number in the rickshaw hierarchy, the *malek*. Once a mysteri owns around seven rickshaws, the business of renting them out overpowers the simple logistics of looking after them. At that point the mysteri becomes a malek, a rickshaw owner on a large scale. A large fleet needs a full-time mysteri, so the new malek hires a mechanic and devotes all his energies to fleet management. Gallagher found that the average mysteri fleet numbered five rickshaws while the average malek owned 18. There were a half-dozen Dhaka maleks with fleets of 400, and although he could never track them down, Gallagher heard stories of 'super-maleks' with fleets of more than 1000.

The path from mysteri to malek is not a straightforward one — there's always the possibility of falling foul of rickshaw thieves on the way. Dhaka's horrendous traffic leads to some horrendous accidents but the danger of having your rickshaw stolen is equally real. Many rickshaw pullers, working hard to ascend the rickshaw ownership ladder, are pushed back to the economic starting line when their vehicle is stolen. And then there are *mastans*, close relations to the rickshaw thieves. These muscle men extort protection money for a mysteri's roadside worksite. If the payments are not made, the police, often in cahoots with the mastans, are likely to seize the mysteri's tools and hold them until a fine is paid. Next time the mastan comes by, the mysteri pays up.

Rickshaw Art

Bangladeshi rickshaws are the most colorful and artistic in the world. A fully decorated, shiny new rickshaw will start out with plastic flowers in jars bolted in front of the handlebars. Streamers and colored tape decorate the bars, the seats are brightly painted, the folding top is vividly embroidered, and the rickshaw body is plated with brilliant chrome, studded and painted.

The *pièce de résistance*, however, is the small panel fixed below the rickshaw body. It appears to be there for purely decorative purposes, to shield the rear axle and chassis parts from public view and give a following rickshaw rider and his passengers something to look at. All sorts of designs and illustrations appear on these panels, and since rickshaw manufacturing is a local and scattered business there are often particular enclaves of the city with their own specialist designs. Close to the Ahsan Manzil museum in Old Dhaka, for example, several rickshaws sport illustrations of card-playing tigers. The most popular panel theme pays homage to the movie world of Bollywood: flanked by plump heroines, long-haired, unshaven heroes stare threateningly back at following traffic. Like film posters, these movie stars are larger-than-life characters, and twice as brightly colored.

Despite their overwhelming numbers and the huge part they play in everyday life, Dhaka's rickshaws are totally uncelebrated. There is little to satisfy an avid rickshaw souvenir hunter – no rickshaw postcards and few rickshaw toys. The Bangsal Rd bicycle shops, however, have every possible rickshaw component, including off-the-shelf rickshaw artwork. Brightly painted metal rear panels, an authentic expression of Bangladeshi folk art, can be bought for $2.50.

Rickshaw Manufacturing — Mysteris . . .

Above
A mysteri, or rickshaw mechanic, paints the axle and rear springs of a rickshaw.

Right
Assembling the vividly decorated seat for a new rickshaw.

Dhaka may have more rickshaws than any other city on earth, but manufacturing them is still a cottage industry. There are no rickshaw assembly lines — in fact rickshaws are pretty much made to order. You zip over to Bangsal Rd, the 'Bicycle St' of Dhaka, collect all the parts that go into making a rickshaw, take them back to your workshop and put them together. It's a simple and unsophisticated process and it produces an equally straightforward end product. Just off Municipal St in the Banglabazar area of Old Dhaka, you'll find a slew of small businesses involved in every stage of rickshaw manufacturing. In hole-in-the-wall workshops, seats are assembled and upholstered, the vinyl tops are stretched over their bamboo bows and complete rickshaws are assembled and painted. In one small courtyard, a family of rickshaw artists paint the purely decorative rear panels.

There are a host of reasons why the production process should remain so undeveloped, even in the country with the world's biggest rickshaw output. A prime one is that the government has actively discouraged rickshaw production. It may seem remarkable, but Bangladesh has higher import duties for bicycles and for the components that go into bicycles and rickshaws than, for example, for motorcycles and cars. Illogical? Well, there was a logical reason behind that illogical result. It's called protection. Nobody was going to manufacture motorcycles or cars in Bangladesh, so there was no local industry which would suffer from imports. There were, however, potentially at least, local bicycle manufacturers to protect, so the government slapped punitive duties on

. . . & Artists

imported bicycle and rickshaw parts. Of course reality hasn't shaped up the way the government planned it: local bicycle manufacturers haven't flourished behind the import barrier, but imported parts are much more expensive than they need be.

The small scale and local nature of rickshaw production, together with the government's negative attitude towards the whole business, have conspired to shackle rickshaw design. Bangladesh may roll out 70,000 new rickshaws every year but their design has scarcely changed since the first three-wheeler made its appearance in the 1930s. There have been a number of projects, some of them enjoying overseas aid funding, aimed at producing a better rickshaw. None of them have enjoyed more than fleeting success. The deficiencies of the current rickshaw design may be easy to pinpoint, but they have proved far from easy to overcome.

Rickshaw art, on the other hand, undergoes constant development. Rickshaw owners may be notoriously tight-fisted but for a classy *ek number* (number one) rickshaw, a quarter of the vehicle's cost will have gone into the art. Mere mysteris, or rickshaw mechanics, may assemble the rickshaw, make and decorate the hood and seat, or paint the frame and mechanical parts, but a rickshaw artist is called in to paint the ornate rear panels.

There have often been crackdowns by the authorities on the wilder expressions of rickshaw art. Perhaps it's a reminder of the first days of the hand-pulled jinrikisha, which had no sooner appeared on the streets of Tokyo than restrictions were in force to limit the salacious paintings with which they were decorated. At first there were no-nonsense rules imposed by the British colonial authorities: rickshaws were to be painted dark blue, their lining was to be red and iron work was to be painted black. The first cycle-rickshaws were equally drab, but with the end of the British era they gradually became more and more colorful.

In 1971, after the split from Pakistan, one of the first rules brought in by the new government of independent Bangladesh enforced restrictions on depictions of unveiled women. Rearview mirrors were also banned on the grounds that rickshaw riders were more likely to be using them to eye their female passengers than to keep an eye on following traffic! In 1978 the authorities decided the movie star paintings were getting out of hand and there was a temporary shift towards city and nature scenes. In 1982 severe restrictions were brought in for the artwork on buses, taxis and baby taxis, but rickshaws escaped that crackdown. It looks likely that Dhaka's rickshaws will roll into the next century unchallenged in their position as the world's gaudiest.

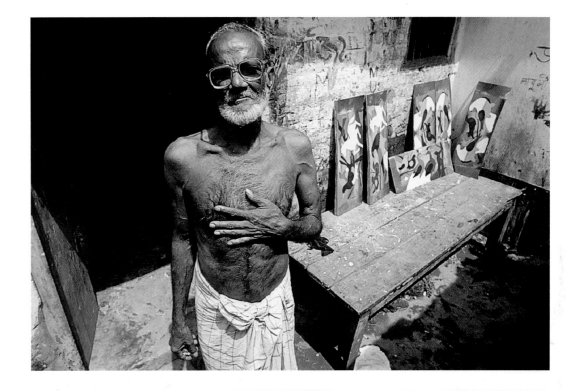

Above
The decorative heart shapes are hung from the back of Dhaka rickshaws.

Right
Ghulam Nabi and his son Yousuf Nabi are rickshaw artists, painting the backboards that decorate every Dhaka rickshaw. Yousuf is 21 years old and has been painting rickshaw panels since he left school.

Above
The wooden offcuts are made into the heart shapes which will be painted, plated and studded to become another part of a rickshaw's gaudy design.

Left
Rickshaw bodies pile up on the riverside while a boatload stands ready to head across the river to supply Dhaka rickshaw builders.

Right
Mujibur Rahman is a young man with a flourishing business on the Buriganga riverbanks, across the river from Old Dhaka. His six young workers turn out 200 wooden rickshaw bodies a day in an operation that takes in whole tree trunks, saws them into planks in one building and turns them into the bodies and seat bases in another. From there they are loaded on to a boat to be paddled across the river and supplied to rickshaw assemblers.

Riverbank Rickshaw Bodies

A Depot & a Dormitory

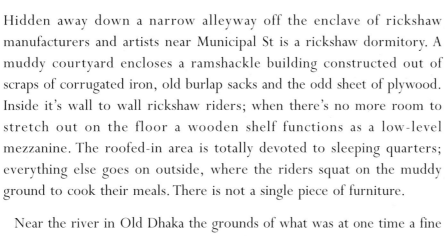

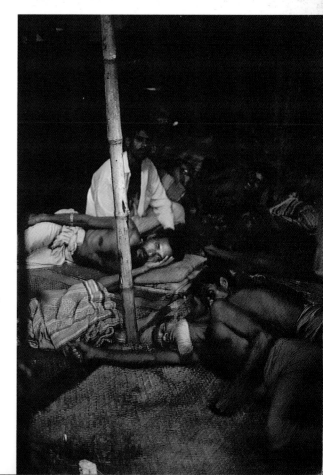

Hidden away down a narrow alleyway off the enclave of rickshaw manufacturers and artists near Municipal St is a rickshaw dormitory. A muddy courtyard encloses a ramshackle building constructed out of scraps of corrugated iron, old burlap sacks and the odd sheet of plywood. Inside it's wall to wall rickshaw riders; when there's no more room to stretch out on the floor a wooden shelf functions as a low-level mezzanine. The roofed-in area is totally devoted to sleeping quarters; everything else goes on outside, where the riders squat on the muddy ground to cook their meals. There is not a single piece of furniture.

Near the river in Old Dhaka the grounds of what was at one time a fine old *rajbari* is now a rickshaw depot. Rajbaris were stately homes, built in the late 19th and early 20th century by the city's Hindu elite, made wealthy by the region's flourishing jute industry. The Hindus have gone and the city's rajbaris are almost all in various states of terminal decay. This one is now a dormitory for the local police station. It's nowhere near as primitive as the rickshaw riders' dormitory but it's still far from luxurious, with several families crammed into each room. A century ago the house might have looked out over a well-kept garden but now it's just a muddy compound crowded with rickshaws where Omar Faruq keeps an eye over his fleet and ticks off each arriving and departing rickshaw in his accounts book.

Left
Rickshaw riders prepare a meal in the muddy courtyard outside their dormitory.

Top right
Rickshaw owner Omar Faruq.

Middle right
Omar Faruq's rickshaw accounts book.

Bottom right
Rickshaw riders stretched out on the floor of their dormitory. Many rickshaw riders are temporary residents in the city, owning nothing more than the clothes they wear.

Bicycle Street

It isn't only the continuous battle to control your own rickshaw-size patch of road which tells the tale of Dhaka's rickshaw population. A stroll down Bangsal Rd will quickly bring home just how many rickshaws the city supports, and how quickly more and more of them are spilling on to the streets. For two whole blocks nearly every shop is dedicated to motorcycles, bicycles and rickshaws. Gleaming new Indian and Chinese versions of Japanese motorcycles edge out on to the roadside, while shop after shop is packed full of gaudy Chinese mountain bikes or conservative Indian single-speed Hero city bikes.

Left
A Bangsal Rd sign for a rickshaw and bicycle parts shop.

Above
Rickshaw wheel hubs.

In between, countless shops supply every bicycle component imaginable, including pretty much every piece you'd need to assemble your own brand-new rickshaw. Sturdy twin-top tube frames are stacked in neat interlocking triangular structures, wheel rims and tires are piled up to the roof, pack after pack of wheel spokes sit ready to be laced into the shiny new wheels. There are heaps of the weighty cast-iron frameworks which connect the bicycle frame to the rear axle and the passenger seat, and rows of rough wooden seat frames await painting, upholstering and plating with silvery chromed sheets. Axles, wheel-bearing housings, saddles, handlebars, brakes, chains, sprockets, pedals and other bits and pieces wait for buyers.

A few years ago the government announced a ban on issuing more new rickshaw licenses, but the volume of parts in Bangsal Rd shops, the countless local manufacturers supplying components to the shops and the numerous small rickshaw assemblers plainly indicate that nothing will stop the Dhaka rickshaw population from growing. The annual rickshaw license fee is only about $5, but since the government stopped issuing new licenses the price for a legal one has escalated to around $150. Two-thirds of the city's rickshaws have dispensed with legality, operating with a fake license or none at all.

The cost of a completely new rickshaw varies considerably, depending on the quality of the components used and even more with the amount of work that goes into the rickshaw's artwork. A straightforward rickshaw can be put on the road for less than $200 but a top-class example might cost 50% more. Fleet owners rent their rickshaws out for around a dollar a day.

Top
Rickshaw parts piled up, appropriately enough, on a rickshaw seat.

Middle
Sprockets, chains, cranks, wheel hubs and other rickshaw parts hang on a bicycle shop wall.

Bottom
Wooden bodies are piled up on bamboo bows for the rickshaw tops.

Hanoi

The Vietnamese capital's one million people live in a city of surprising beauty. The American bombing of the 1960s and 1970s seems to have had remarkably little impact on the city itself and the slow pace of postwar development has helped to preserve the city's French colonial charm. In the last few years Hanoi has started to emulate its fast-living southern sister, Saigon, but high-rise construction has yet to encroach on the colorful streets of the city's Old Quarter. In fact one of the most visible signs of Hanoi's 20th-century catch-up has been the arrival of charming little cafés along the old city's shady, tree-lined avenues. The cycle-rickshaw or cyclo would seem to be the perfect transport for this cityscape but Hanoi's cycle-rickshaws are actually on the retreat, as is evidenced by the proliferation of 'No Rickshaw' signs all over the city center. Unlike in other Asian cities, it's not four-wheeled transport which is pushing the cycle-rickshaw towards extinction: Hanoi is simply overwhelmed by two-wheelers. Bicycles and motorcycles monopolize the traffic; the public transport role of the cycle-rickshaw has been grabbed not by buses and taxis but by motorcycles, which hang round every major intersection waiting for fare-paying passengers to perch on the pillion seats.

Cyclo Design

Like the trishaws of Penang and the becaks of Yogyakarta, the cyclos of Hanoi put passengers out front while the rider pedals along behind. Braking is only on the rear wheel and consists of a drum with an external shoe operated by pulling a lever. It feels truly horrible, makes lots of noise and doesn't appear

Left
Puffing on a cigarette and sporting a Viet Cong-style helmet, Hoang looks every inch the typical Hanoi cyclo pilot.

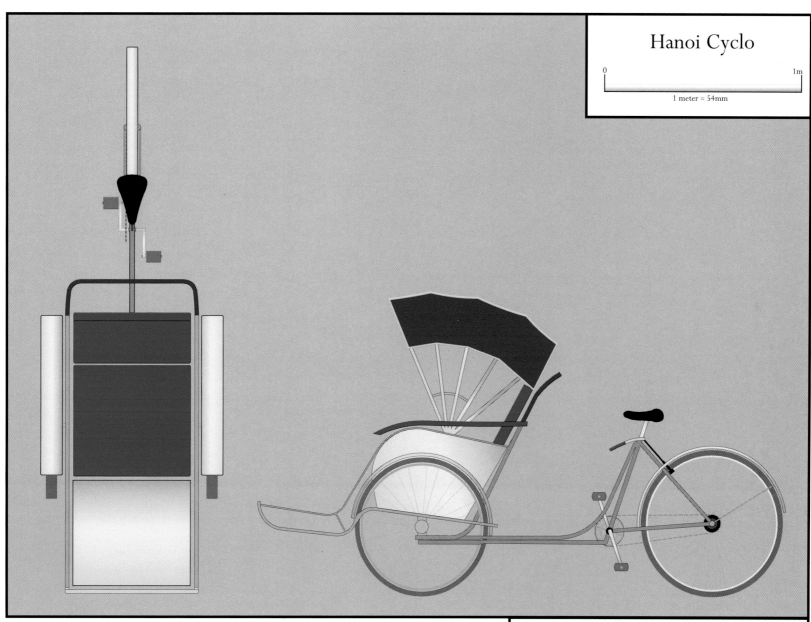

Hanoi Cyclo

0 ————————————————— 1m

1 meter = 54mm

to provide any retardation at all! Saigon cyclos, which are narrower, are only capable of carrying one person; Hanoi cyclos can certainly carry two, although passengers are cramped for space, and are quite luxurious for just one. If Saigon cyclos are sports cars, the Hanoi ones are station wagons.

number of cyclos in city	2000	
weight	253 lbs	115 kg
wheelbase	59 inches	150 cm
overall length	105 inches	266 cm
track	33 inches	84 cm
overall width	37 inches	95 cm
passenger seat width	23 inches	59 cm
front wheels diameter	26 inches	68 cm
rear wheel diameter	28 inches	72 cm
front tire size	26 x 1.5 inches	
rear tire size	28 x 1.5 inches	

To Market

Cyclos are regular visitors to Hanoi's colorful markets, delivering produce or taking shoppers home with their purchases. The city's cyclos are arbitrarily divided into two categories — tourist cyclos and market cyclos. The market variety tend to be rough and ready, more suitable for conveying sacks of onions or baskets of squawking chickens than fussy passengers.

Left
In the dim, dawn hours of a rainy day at Dong Xuan Market on the edge of the historic Old Quarter of Hanoi sacks of vegetables are hauled off a heavily loaded cyclo. The vegetables in Vietnam's produce markets always look appetisingly fresh.

Top

There's no way the cyclo rider could see over this shaky tower of wooden crates but Hanoi's market cyclos are equipped with two handles so that the rider can forsake riding and start pulling.

Bottom

A large flock of ducks peer around from their cyclo transport. They've just crossed the Long Bien Bridge across the Song Hong or Red River, on their way to Dong Xuan Market. A prime target for American B-52s during the Vietnam War, the bridge was often damaged and to this day shows the signs of a long chain of haphazard and hurried repairs. Bicycles and motorcycles comprise most of the bridge traffic; there's the occasional cyclo but cars are strictly forbidden.

Cyclo Repairs

Long runs a pavement repair depot with his wife, Ha. It means working outside, but there's no rent to pay. Long's been at it for 10 years, typically doing minor repairs or changing tires. While we were talking to Long, Duong came along with a white cyclo with a broken spring. He told us he was 47, had five children and had been riding cyclos for six years. Previously, he had been mining for gold!

Left
The cyclo's rear brake is operated by an external brake shoe which makes lots of noise but doesn't work very well.

Above
Duong watches Long repair his cyclo.

Right
A stylish wooden cyclo pedal.

Cyclo Economics

Most riders own their own cyclos these days. In the past they used to rent them from fleet owners who would have typically had just four or five vehicles. A cyclo can be bought for around $200, and the annual license costs about $30. Riders usually make about $2.50 a day but big-spending tourists can soon bump that up.

There are 6000 cyclos in Hanoi and about 60,000 cars but they're both comprehensively outnumbered by the city's huge population of two-wheelers. The bicycles and motorcycles number in the hundreds of thousands and as a result the traffic never seems to stop – at intersections the flow in one direction simply merges and passes through the cross flow. Nobody ever comes to a halt.

Left
As the 'No Entry' signs indicate, cyclos are banned
from many streets in the center of Hanoi.

Above
A rainy day cyclo speeds along Hang Quat St in the
Old Quarter of Hanoi.

Left
Grandmother, mother and daughter are pedaled through Hanoi's Old Quarter.

Right
Traffic is increasingly being restricted in Hanoi's Old Quarter.

Cyclo Manufacturing

Above
Technical section manager Vu Tri Thuc stands beside a
new cyclo chassis-frame.

There does not appear to be any cycle-rickshaw manufacturing in Hanoi itself, although there are plenty of small repair depots. The Coloa Mechanical Factory in Dong Anh, 20-odd km out of Hanoi towards the airport, occasionally turns out batches of new cyclos to order. When we visited they'd just finished a batch of 60, which displayed some improvements over old-style cyclos, including an axle located by leading links and suspended by motorcycle-style coil springs and shock absorbers. Vu Tri Thuc, manager of the technical section, explained that the cyclos are delivered as a chassis-frame. The purchaser still has to trim them and fit the bicycle components like the sprockets, wheels, saddle and trim.

The 'Arrested' Depot

Cyclos are brought to the riverside 'arrested cyclos' depot after they've been seized by the police. A cyclo might be seized because it's old and unroadworthy, because its rider has broken some traffic regulation or because it's a cyclo from the provinces which has been ridden in Hanoi without the proper license. Eventually the cyclos are destroyed. Nam 5 is the manager of the 'arrested' depot.

Hong Kong

Economic mega-city, meeting point of east and west, site of some of the world's most expensive real estate, home to one of the world's most profitable subway systems, vendor of more Rolls-Royces per capita than just about anywhere, Hong Kong seems like the last place on earth to find hand-pulled rickshaws. The Hong Kong rickshaw may be close to breathing its last and its role today may be almost pure tourist icon, but it has had a long and colorful history in the city. Hong Kong was a pioneering city in the rickshaw's spread across Asia and it soon became a vital form of transport, particularly in the crowded Hong Kong Central business area. Then taxis and prosperity pushed the rickshaw off the road and today it is clearly an endangered species.

Rickshaw Design

It seems strange to say that a rickshaw has a more modern design, but Hong Kong's last handful of rickshaws are undeniably more modern than their Calcutta equivalents. Their wheels have steel spokes, for example, while the Calcutta rickshaw still has wooden wheels.

Left
Lui Luk was born in 1928 and has been pulling rickshaws since 1947, back when they served as practical transport. In those days, before taxis and buses made a complete takeover, he would take passengers anywhere in Hong Kong Central for just a few cents.
   'When did the change from transport to tourist icon take place?' I inquired.
   'Change?' replied Lui Luk. 'Never. You get in my rickshaw now and I will take you anywhere in Central.'
   It would be a very expensive way of getting there.

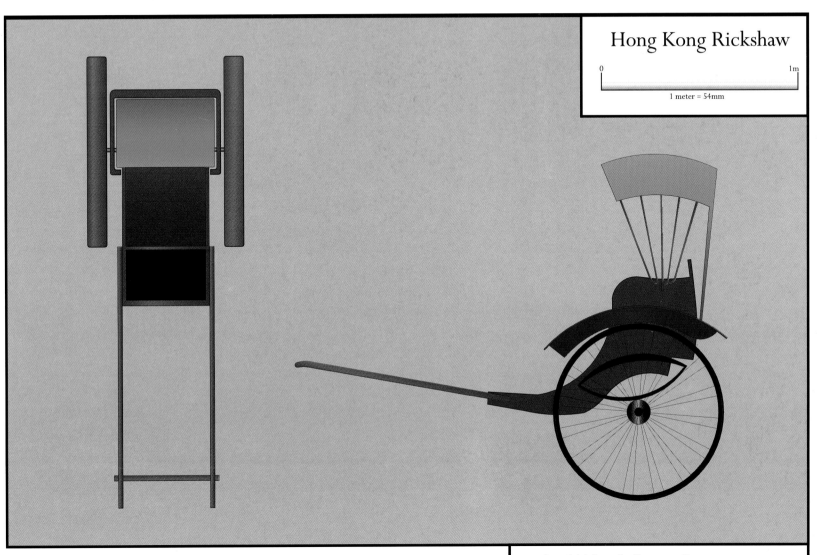

Hong Kong Rickshaw

0   1m

1 meter = 54mm

number of rickshaws in city	8	
weight	132 lbs	60 kg
overall length	91 inches	230 cm
track	29 inches	74 cm
overall width	31 inches	80 cm
passenger seat width	20 inches	50 cm
wheel diameter	35 inches	88 cm

Where Have All the Rickshaws Gone?

Rickshaws must have appeared in Hong Kong soon after their invention as the Japanese jinrikisha. By 1895 there were already 700 registered, licensed rickshaws in the colony and there were probably more than 5000 during WW I. In the mid-1920s, despite competition from buses, trams and other mechanized transport, they still numbered more than 3000 and were a vital part of the colony's transport network. Over the next 15 years rickshaws dwindled away until there were only a few hundred left at the start of WW II, but their numbers must have swollen dramatically during the war and in the tough years that followed because there were about 8000 registered in the late 1940s. This peak was followed by a rapid decline, as taxis and increased traffic congestion swept rickshaws off the roads in the 1950s and 1960s. By the early 1970s rickshaws had ceased to be a means of transport and had become a pure and simple tourist attraction.

It's said the last license was issued in 1975, when there were nearly 100 rickshaws left in the colony, but the rickshaw pullers still seem to have current licenses that cost them HK$50 a year. Although there is no campaign to get rid of rickshaws, the remaining rickshaw 'boys' are now old men and ready to entertain offers from any collector who might care to buy their steeds.

At their height, rickshaws were not simply used as public transport. Businesses and well-off families often kept a rickshaw, much as they would a car today. Towards the end of WW I there were even 60 rickshaws registered in the name of brothels; they were used to deliver courtesans to their customers.

During the Vietnam R&R years of the 1960s and into the 1970s rickshaws could be found on both the Hong Kong Island and Kowloon side of the Star Ferry run and there was a busy trade to the bars and brothels of Wanchai. By the early 1980s rickshaws numbered fewer than 50 and they eventually contracted to the small group which still hangs out at the Star Ferry pier on the Hong Kong Island side, waiting to take visitors on a short jog around the car park or to pose for photographs. There were less than 20 left in the early 1990s and when we turned up in late 1997 they were truly an endangered species; just eight rickshaws remained and the 'For Sale' sign hung suspended above the whole collection indicated that their days are truly numbered.

Left
In 1997 there were only eight rickshaws left in Hong Kong. Here are five of them.

Right
Rickshaws on Connaught Rd Central.

Left
Chan Chau has been pulling rickshaws for 10 to 15 years and remembers that there were still 30 left in Central when he started.

Right
Born in Hong Kong in 1936, Lam Ping Keun used to work as a watchman at a fire station. He has been pulling rickshaws for 15 years but only as a tourist business – rickshaws had ceased to be everyday transport by the time he acquired his. A 'For Sale' sign hangs over his rickshaw number 4.

Above
Hong Kong rickshaw licenses.

Right
Hong Kong's last rickshaw pullers line up behind Chan Mok, a rickshaw puller for 10 to 15 years.

Macau

Only 65 km west of Hong Kong, on the other side of the Pearl River estuary, Macau is a laidback Portuguese version of its businesslike neighbor. In recent years Macau has also become a major manufacturing center, land reclamation has dramatically increased the city's size and skyscrapers now tower over the old colonial buildings, but it's still a quiet backwater in comparison to frenetic Hong Kong. The city's small cycle-rickshaw fleet, known as *triciclos*, are completely in tune with the Macau lifestyle. They're spacious, comfortable and more suitable for lazy cruising than for getting anywhere in a hurry. The triciclos are almost totally dedicated to the tourist business. Since gambling is one of Macau's major preoccupations, it's appropriate that most of its triciclos can be found lined up outside the garish Hotel Lisboa, home to the city's largest casino.

Triciclo Design

Macau's rickshaws are heavy but have very wide and comfortable seats – only the Beijing version approaches their lounge-back seating width. Technologically the triciclo is quite advanced, with brakes on all three wheels. The front brake is operated by a standard rod system from the front handlebar lever, while the rear wheels are worked by rod-operated brakes linked to a single foot-operated lever that requires you to take your right foot off the pedal – rather like the system in Penang but more sophisticated in the brake itself.

The Macau rickshaws also have two-speed gears operated by hand using a lever on the top tube. It's a rather Heath Robinson arrangement: the front chain

Left
Triciclo repairs outside the Hotel Lisboa. The double chain on the primary and secondary axles can be seen on the right-hand side.

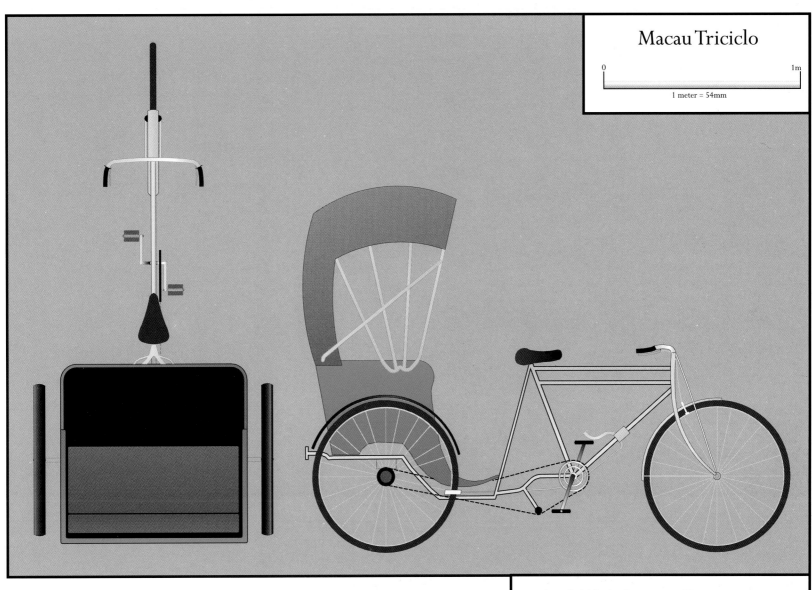

Macau Triciclo

0   1m

1 meter = 54mm

number of triciclos in city	50	
weight	271 lbs	123 kg
wheelbase	67 inches	169 cm
overall length	100 inches	253 cm
track	41 inches	104 cm
overall width	48 inches	122 cm
passenger seat width	33 inches	84 cm
wheel diameter	28 inches	72 cm
tire size	28 x 1.5 inches	

drives a secondary axle with two sprockets, each of which is connected to a sprocket on the primary axle. So the system has a primary chain (and two sprockets) and two secondary chains (each with two sprockets): a total of three chains and six sprockets for just two gears. But the actual change seems to work well, and although the lower gear is very low indeed the riders seem to use both ratios quite regularly. Macau is fairly hilly but the triciclo riders stick to the flat bits.

How Many Triciclos?

Triciclos all carry a three-figure registered number from LS-1 up. Since the highest number we saw was 172 there couldn't be more than 200 left at the outside, and I'd estimate there were actually only about 50 in use. Quite a few triciclos sit around looking rather derelict; there's a collection of rusting triciclos by the ferry building and more of them lined up at the Hotel Lisboa than can possibly be needed.

Left
A rider lounges in his triciclo in front of the Hotel Lisboa.

Top right
Selector lever for a Macau triciclo's two-speed gearing.

Middle & bottom right
Year of manufacture and license plate.

Far right
Triciclo parking.

RUA
OESTE DO
MERCADO DE
S. DOMINGOS

公局新市西街

TRICICLOS

三輪車站

Triciclos in Use

Although triciclos get a minor commercial workout delivering produce to the markets, Macau's rickshaws exist almost exclusively for tourist use and then in a decidedly lackadaisical fashion. Macau tourism is predominantly confined to the casinos, so there isn't a great deal of sightseeing tourism and the rickshaw riders pursue it very half-heartedly. They simply sit and wait for the tourists to come to them and then don't seem very interested in being friendly or tourist minded.

Occasionally a triciclo may hang around the Largo do Senado square in the center, but mostly they congregate at the Hotel Lisboa, where they wait in line to be hailed. The riders have a three-part fixed-price list – $9 for a 20-minute tour, $11 for 30 minutes, $20 for an hour. They've certainly priced themselves right out of the local transport market.

Above
A triciclo framed in the arcades of the Largo do Senado square.

Right
Macau map and triciclo tour price list.

Far right
A triciclo in front of the A-Ma Temple.

Manila

The mega-city capital of the Philippines, Manila has a population of 10 million and a transport system dominated by the jeepney. These exuberantly decorated descendants of WW II American jeeps are the number one way of getting around. Clogging every street in the city and colorfully decorated, they seem to go hand in hand with the Filipino attitude to life — convivial, noisy and lived to the limit. With jeepneys jammed hubcap to hubcap it seems scarcely credible that Manila could offer space for another transport system, but get off the main roads and into the local neighborhoods and you'll find the city's sidecars, often so gaudily turned out that they look like junior versions of their four-wheeled brethren.

Sidecar Design

Despite their toylike appearance Filipino sidecars are remarkably well designed. The BMX-size bicycle is rigidly bolted on to the sidecar, so it doesn't suffer from the un-nerving flexing and wandering of, say, the Burmese sidecar design. Although the gearing is very low — these are definitely short-distance vehicles — that's partly balanced by the machine's incredible maneuverability. A Manila sidecar is short but wide and can turn corners so sharply it will literally reverse direction at a flick of the handlebars. Despite its compact size the sidecar itself is also surprisingly roomy: you can squeeze two adult passengers in relatively easily, and many sidecars have a small rear-facing bench seat at the front, an ideal perch for a couple of young children. There's even room for bags and shopping under or behind the seat.

Left
Putting the finishing touches to brand-new sidecars.

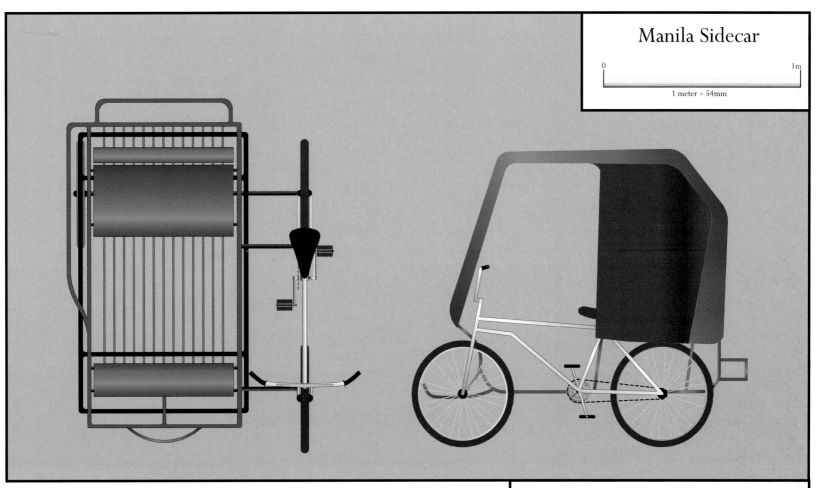

0   1m

1 meter = 54mm

All this compact design and relatively light weight disappears out the window in the full stereo sidecar. The nearest thing to a three-wheeled jeepney with pedals, the full stereo sidecar is bedecked with lights, horns and, of course, stereo equipment. Throw in a frequently recharged car battery to power all this equipment and it can easily add 100 lbs (45 kg) to a regular sidecar's 200 lb (90 kg) weight.

number of sidecars in city	2000	
weight	200 lbs	90 kg
wheelbase	40 inches	102 cm
overall length	72 inches	182 cm
track	40 inches	102 cm
overall width	54 inches	136 cm
passenger seat width	28 inches	70 cm
wheel diameter	20 inches	52 cm
tire size	20 x 2.125 inches	

Nino Quilon's Full Stereo Sidecar

Nino Quilon's Full Stereo Sidecar

Nino Quilon's sidecar sports four lights and three horns on the roof, while three yellow lights, three white lights, three blue lights and two red lights are plastered across the front. There are also the inevitable rearview mirrors (so useful for straightening your hair if not for watching following traffic) and a little collection of plastic pot plants. Inside, the space under the seat is occupied by twin 12-inch (30-cm) speakers blasting out a thumping rap beat. The sidecar is even lower geared than normal, for Nino has a passenger weight of equipment on board even before the first fare-paying passenger climbs in. It also costs more per day to rent his fancy sidecar.

So why carry round all this extra junk and pay more for it as well? The answer is obvious: while other riders lounge on their regular sidecars, waiting for a fare, the full stereo machines roll by time after time with yet another passenger on board. They simply attract more business.

If rickshaw jockeys in other cities are frequently the superannuated elderly, who often look like they'll soon be heading to some rickshaw park in the sky, many of Manila's riders look as if they've sneaked out of school for the day. Perhaps Manila's sidecars are simply a training ground for the occupation which every red-blooded Filipino male really covets: jeepney driver. The youthful riders, combined with the toytown appearance of the Filipino sidecar design, make the vehicles look more like playthings than serious transport. Sidecars are also known as pedicabs or, colloquially, as a *padjak*, a slang Tagalog (Pilipino) expression that means something like 'kick' or 'push' or 'kick on out of here'. The word 'tricycle' is reserved for motorcycles with sidecars, which are also a popular means of transport in the Philippines.

The vast majority of sidecar riders rent their vehicles, typically paying about $2 a day. The sidecar fleets are generally very small. A typical fleet consists of only three or four machines, although some have up to 10 and in the San Paulo district of the city a group of owners run a fleet of 50. Established riders have regular customers and control the best positions by the markets; newcomers have to pick up the crumbs.

Sidecars & Their Youthful Riders

Above
Even for Manila these two riders – Edgar Pineda Junior and Peter Agil – are very young. Edgar on the right is 14; Peter is only 13. They attend school from 6 am to 12 noon and then ride their sidecars until late at night. They told us that the police had just taken the seat cushions from their sidecars because they'd been blocking the rush-hour traffic near the market. They were immobilised and would have to pay to get the cushions back.

Above
Collecting school children from Our Lady of Carmel School.

Right
Thirty-eight-year-old Rocky Berliot has been riding for five years. He owns his sidecar and on a typical day makes $6 to $7; not having to pay a couple of dollars rental out of that take makes life much easier. Rocky thinks riding a sidecar is much better than being a construction worker. The money is similar, but sidecar riders have much more freedom and don't face the serious risk of accidents and injury on a building site.

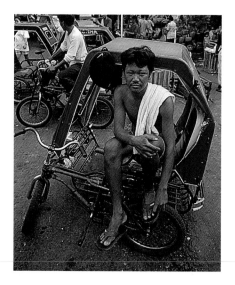

Above
In all of Asia we only met two women rickshaw riders, one in Beijing and one in Manila. Baby Delavin is 23 years old and has been pedaling a sidecar for 18 months. She reckons it is tough work, hard on the legs. Baby is the only woman rider working in the Quiapo Market district, although she thinks there are several other female riders in Manila.

Left
'Chickboy' it proclaims across the back of this full stereo sidecar; the slang Manila expression indicates the young rider, Faisal Lucas, is a bit of a playboy.

A Sidecar Manufacturer

Shiela Gulapa, the sidecar-manufacturing business in Manila's Tondo district run by Boy Gulapa and his wife, Conne, rolls out 150 sidecars a year. Johnjohn Norias, the company's ace mechanic, is just 15 years old. A brand-new sidecar sells for about $250; you can spend another $80 on a heavy-duty version, complete with bigger bearings and heavier tubing. The welding, painting and assembly all takes place in the Gulapa's busy little establishment, while an adjacent hole-in-the-wall shop stitches up seat covers and tops.

Left
Ray Alcaras fits studs to a new sidecar's seating upholstery.

Above
Johnjohn in his cardboard-and-sunglasses welding mask.

Right
Sidecar manufacturers Boy and Conne Gulapa.

Penang

Officially the city of Penang doesn't exist. Penang is the island off the north-west coast of Malaysia, while the city on the north-east corner of Penang Island is Georgetown. Nevertheless everybody refers to the latter as Penang and it's a city remarkable for its stiff resistance to change. Yes, Penang Island is a center for Malaysia's high-tech computer businesses and yes, they've plonked the ugly 60-story Komtar skyscraper right in the middle of the old town, but most of the town center has managed to stay virtually unchanged since the early years of this century. If you wonder what Singapore was like in the 1950s, before the government embarked on the wholesale demolition of the old Chinese shopfronts with their charming design and semi-enclosed pedestrian walkways known as the 'five foot ways', you need only travel 1000 km north to Penang. The city's population is less than a quarter of a million and cycle-rickshaw numbers are small and declining, but they still play an active part in everyday life. Sure they're a tourist attraction — and the riders are quite used to playing the part of tour conductor — but they're equally at home conveying housewives back from the market, laden with fresh fruit and vegetables.

Trishaw Design

In Singapore, and most other cities on the Malay Peninsula, trishaws are basically bicycles with sidecars attached, but Georgetown favors the Indonesian style with rider behind and passengers in front. In comparison to the dumpy becaks of Yogyakarta, however, the Penang trishaws are longer, lower and more sporty looking. From an engineering viewpoint, they are probably Asia's most elegant cycle-rickshaws.

Left
Zainul Abidin Mahmud came from Kedah to Penang and took up trishaw riding a year ago. Like many trishaw riders he lives in his vehicle but, unlike the vast majority of them, he is not a bachelor. Zainul has a wife and two daughters, aged four months and two years, and they shelter in a 'five foot way' across from the Kapitan Kling Mosque.

Penang Trishaw

0   1m

1 meter = 54mm

number of trishaws in city	400	
weight	275 lbs	125 kg
wheelbase	55 inches	140 cm
overall length	108 inches	275 cm
track	38 inches	96 cm
overall width	42 inches	107 cm
passenger seat width	26 inches	66 cm
wheel diameter	28 inches	72 cm
tire size	28 x 1.5 inches	

Above
A full trishaw load of vegetables snakes through the streets of Georgetown.

Jinrikisha to Trishaw

Above
The enameled plate proclaiming that it's a 'Jinrikisha 1st Class' is a valuable indicator of a vintage Penang trishaw's authenticity.

The Malaysian cycle-rickshaw is known as the trishaw or *trisha*, an invented word made from combining 'tricycle' with 'rickshaw', much as the machine is a combination of bicycle and rickshaw. Perhaps to underline the Japanese connection each trishaw carries an ancient-looking, circular, green or blue-enameled license plate with the word 'Jinrikisha', the original Japanese term for their hand-pulled invention, above the vehicle's license number and '1st Class' below.

As the hand-pulled jinrikisha was a Japanese invention, the vehicles were a target during anti-Japanese riots which took place in Penang in 1919. However, it was the Japanese who finished them off – it was during their occupation of Penang that the new-fangled trishaw came into its own. Despite this nod to Japanese influence, it's an open question if the invention can be credited to the Japanese forces who occupied Penang during WW II or to simple expediency, a solution to the wartime transport shortage. Although the hand-pulled rickshaws started to disappear during the war and trishaws took their place, there were certainly three-wheeled bicycles used for transporting goods before the war and quite possibly trishaws as well. Whatever the story of its birth, the trishaw is also known by the Malaysian/Indonesian description becak or *beca* or, less commonly, as a *lanca*.

In 1946, the first year records were kept after WW II, there were already more than 1500 public trishaws in use and the 2000 pre-war rickshaws had dwindled to 600. By 1950 there were more than 2000 registered trishaws but from that point no new licenses were issued. By the early 1970s the number of registered vehicles had fallen to around 1500 and in 1997 there were only 512 registered trishaws left (although many more unregistered ones lie derelict). Remarkably, a handful of the old rickshaws survived long after the arrival of the trishaw; seven of them were still registered in Penang in 1962.

Trishaw People

It's too dangerous an occupation to get married, announced long-time trishaw rider David Kok, aged 54. He went on to estimate that 95% of the city's riders were bachelors, many of them living in their trishaws and sheltering in the 'five foot ways' when it rains. Some view trishaw riders as the lowest rung of society, earning even less than mobile food stall operators, but the Trishaw Riders Association, which runs the nightly trishaw tours of the city, is efficient and businesslike. One of the association's organisers turned up to collect his trishaw on a motorcycle with his mobile phone at his belt, ready to check the tour bus arrival times.

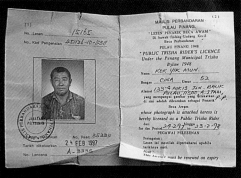

Top
Henry Koh works for the Georgetown city council as a Vehicle Inspector specializing in non-motorized vehicles, which means the city's trishaws and their riders come under his aegis. Each month five or six trishaw riders are put through their test for a trishaw operator's license. Would-be trishaw jockeys, who must provide a medical fitness certificate, have to pedal Mr Koh around the block as he checks their understanding of traffic rules and regulations.

Middle
David Kok's trishaw riding license.

Bottom
Lifting the seat of David's trishaw reveals a rider's whole world.

Ride a Trishaw

'The brake is most important,' repeated trishaw pilot David Kok for the tenth time as I pedaled 1st Class Jinrikisha Number 1606 around the car park behind City Hall, which was empty on a Sunday afternoon.

The brake didn't actually have much braking to offer – imagine stopping your bicycle if it weighed 260 lbs (117 kg) instead of 25 lbs (11.25 kg), had two passengers on board and you were only allowed to use the brake on the rear wheel. Worse still, it requires a very conscious effort to use the brake: you have to take a foot off the pedals – in fact both feet would probably be better – and stand heavily on the brake pedal.

Slowing down may not come naturally but it doesn't take too much effort either because trishaws rarely move fast. Lazily loping along is more the order of the day and surprisingly that doesn't require great exertion, even with passengers aboard. David, clearly a connoisseur of trishaw nuances, explained that his trishaw has a 22-tooth rear sprocket, making it much easier to pedal than the high-speed 20-tooth sprocket.

Unlike some cycle-rickshaw designs, the Penang trishaw also feels quite stable and taking corners presents no difficulty; perhaps that's due to the long, low-slung design of the Penang machine, particularly in comparison to the similarly designed Yogyakarta version. The Penang design does have an in-built problem, however, and David pointed out the importance of deploying the front stand before taking on or letting off passengers – otherwise a heavy passenger stepping on the very front end of the trishaw could tip it right over.

The car park behind City Hall on Jalan Tun Syed Sheh was a good place for my trishaw test ride because this is where new trishaw riders must take their 'riding exam'. Every four months each trishaw has to come back here for a roadworthiness check and renewal of its operating license. Once a year a trishaw rider must also renew his license.

Right
In easy-going Georgetown a trishaw rider takes a break while another trishaw, with passengers aboard, pedals down Lebuh Chulia.

The School Trishaw Service

In affluent Malaysia school children are likely to arrive at school on the back of dad's Honda motorcycle or in mum's Mercedes, but plenty of trishaws still do a daily school run. A contract to convey school kids back and forth can bring in $5 a month and an artfully packed trishaw can fit as many as eight small children!

Above & Right
Rickshaws often double as school buses. Penang trishaws deliver a contingent of neatly dressed schoolgirls for their morning lessons.

No New Trishaws

No new trishaw licenses are being issued in George-town and few young riders are taking up the profession, so as the current elderly band of trishaw jockeys die off the fleet is contracting. Some observers say there are as many as 1000 trishaws still plying the streets, while others insist that numbers have fallen as low as 250; the real figure is probably around 400 to 500. Most of the town's riders rent their trishaws, typically paying about a dollar a day.

Although the skills and the equipment for building new trishaws still exist, nobody is making them any more. A brand-new trishaw would probably sell for around $1000 and there simply isn't enough money in the trishaw business to make that sort of investment worthwhile. If you want a trishaw it's possible to pick one up in good condition for around $400 and you could knock $50 off that price if you were willing to forgo the much-prized 'Jinrikisha – 1st Class' license plate.

Alternatively, you could buy a well-worn trishaw and have it rebuilt. Choo Yew Choon runs Hup Huat, a small workshop at 399 Lebuh Chulia, the busy street of small hotels, bars, restaurants and all manner of little shops and businesses which is the budget traveler's center of Georgetown. Here trishaws are repaired and restored – whether it's rewelding a frame or respoking a wheel. For about $600, Mr Choo will find a solid trishaw and in two weeks strip it down, replace the wheels, tires, pedals, bearings and other wearable components, retrim the seat and top, respray it and prepare it for the road.

Above
Choo Yew Choon, Penang's trishaw restorer.

Left
Rebuilding a trishaw wheel in the Hup Huat workshop.

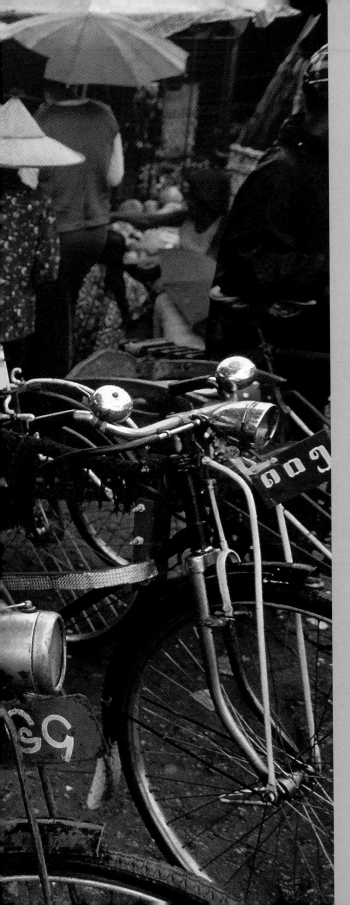

Rangoon

In the past decade Asian progress has finally caught up with Rangoon (or Yangon, as the unpopular and unelected government of Burma [Myanmar] would have it) but it's nevertheless a relatively slow-moving city. It feels far smaller than its four million population would indicate and Rangoon architecture is still redolent of the English colonial period; much of it also looks as if it hasn't seen a paintbrush since that time. Like other Asian cities, Rangoon had a long flirtation with the hand-pulled rickshaw before the *sai kaa*, or cycle-rickshaw, arrived just prior to WW II. Today the sai kaa has been banned from the city center itself, at least during most of the daytime hours, but it's still a vital means of transport in the area immediately around the center and in the suburbs. Burma's interpretation of the cycle-rickshaw is unique: a bicycle with sidecar where the passengers sit back to back.

Sai Kaa Design

The name 'sai kaa' is a Burmese derivation of the English 'sidecar', as sai kaa design was inspired by the motorcycle sidecars which the British army used in Burma during the 1930s. However, the Burmese design, with its back-to-back passenger seating, is unique. The sai kaa is narrow and light but also very basic – it's simply a standard bike with the sidecar bolted on to one side. Wooden blocks are used to join the two parts together and from an engineering point of view this is clearly unsatisfactory. The whole flimsy contraption flexes and wriggles and feels horribly unstable to ride – despite which, sai kaa riders zip along at great speed, perhaps because their machines are very light by rickshaw standards.

Left
A sai kaa rider, wearing a traditional *longyi*, the sarong-like unisex Burmese attire, sits in his sidecar.

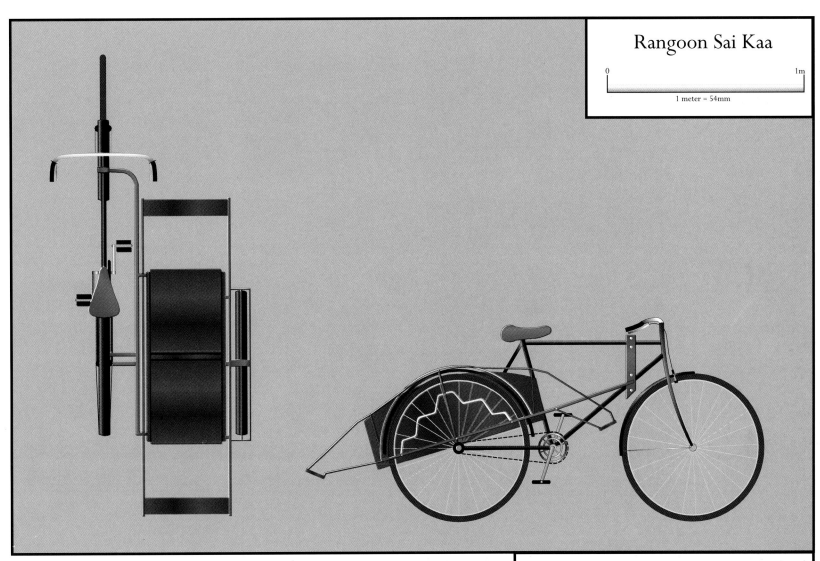

Rangoon Sai Kaa

0   1m

1 meter = 54mm

number of sai kaas in city	7000	
weight	185 lbs	73 kg
wheelbase	46 inches	118 cm
overall length	90 inches	228 cm
track	27 inches	68 cm
overall width	45 inches	115 cm
passenger seat width (2 seats)	14 inches	36 cm
wheel diameter	28 inches	72 cm
tire size	28 x 1.5 inches	

Left or Right?

Burma is not a place where normal logic applies. Until 1970 the Burmese drove on the left, like England and like their neighbors to the west (India and Bangladesh) and to the east (Thailand and Laos). Then the rules were suddenly changed and the Burmese took to driving on the right. It made no sense at all: firstly, because the country was completely isolated, so it made no difference which side the Burmese drove on; secondly, because if the government ever did open the land borders to Thailand (the most likely place) the two countries would be driving on opposite sides; and thirdly, because almost every vehicle in Burma was a venerable relic from the 'British days', with its steering wheel on the right.

The switch makes no better sense today. The current fleet of cars on Burmese roads is much larger and more modern but most of them are second-hand vehicles imported from Japan, which, like Britain and most of the other countries of South-East Asia, drives on the left. The huge number of taxis now circulating around Rangoon are also enjoying a second life, having all clocked up many fares on the streets of Bangkok, Singapore or Tokyo – all cities where you drive on the left.

Left
Chairman of the Sai Kaa Association in the city's Hlaing Ward, U Tan Wai is now semi-retired and devotes his time to being a temple guardian on the platform of the Shwedagon Pagoda. He started out as a rider and has been involved with sai kaas ever since the Japanese occupation during WW II. Today he still owns two sai kaas, down from a few years ago when he had five.

Far left
Sai kaas and their riders line up for passengers arriving at the ferry wharf across from the Strand Hotel.

Why did this utterly pointless change take place? Because, so it is said, Ne Win, Burma's long-term socialist dictator (1962 to 1988), would make no move without consulting his astrologers and fortune-tellers. When he asked them what he could do to improve Burma's collapsing economy they were fearful of directly advising the dictator to retreat from his disastrous 'Burmese Road to Socialism'. So they obliquely suggested that he temper his leftist policies and move to the right. Ne Win promptly commanded that Burmese traffic move from the left-hand side of the road to the right.

Sai kaa design hardly seems to have changed from the day the first one rolled on to a Burmese road in around 1937, but the switch from one side of the road to the other did prompt a wholesale change of side for the sidecars relative to the bicycle. U Ba Kyi of the Pagan Book House reminisced to us about an earlier change of design. Because Buddhists consider the feet the lowest part of the body, for sai kaa passengers to display them was once considered very tasteless. So it is said that the first Mandalay sai kaas were equipped with beautiful, boatlike bodies.

Sai Kaa Decoration, Sai Kaa Fashions

Rangoon's cycle-rickshaws are utilitarian devices but there's still room for some decoration, whether it's colorful stop signs at the back or a reflective warning triangle bolted on the side. There is, however, almost universal agreement that the only appropriate color for a sidecar is red. The appropriate attire for pedaling a sidecar is also standardized: Western trousers have had minimal impact on Burma and for sidecar riders the unisex, sarong-like longyi is the only way to go. Headgear of some kind is also necessary; although anything from an old army helmet to a modern baseball cap will do the job, most riders opt for a Burmese cane version of the Raj-era pith helmet.

Top left
A woman and her child shelter from the rain as they leave the market.

Bottom left
A warning triangle adds style to a Rangoon sai kaa.

Right
A sai kaa rider models the favored headwear.

Above
With passengers and purchases on board the rider
pedals away from the market.

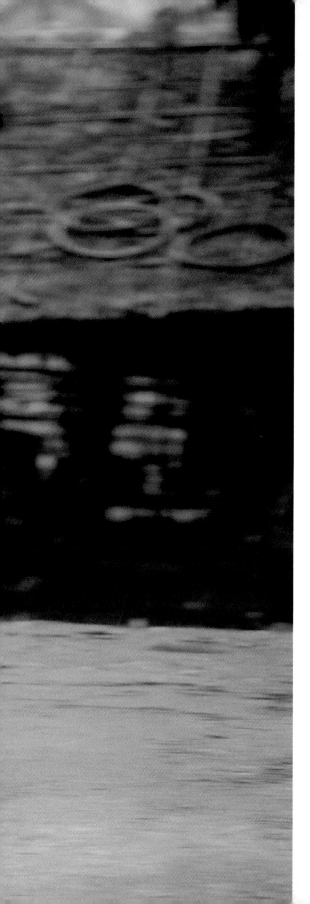

Sai Kaas at Work

Their umbrellas up, two sai kaa passengers are whisked home from the market. It's typical of the stripped-down, spartan nature of the Rangoon sai kaa that this was the one cycle-rickshaw design we encountered with absolutely no weather protection for the passengers. Most riders rent their sai kaa, typically paying between 20 and 40 cents a day for a 6 am to 7 pm shift. An average sai kaa fleet would number about 10 vehicles. As in many other Asian countries the riders are often outsiders – usually squatters from the surrounding countryside. Riders generally make $2 or $3 a day, before paying their rent. The army runs a handy sideline providing safe overnight storage for sai kaas; it costs about 5 cents to store your sai kaa overnight in the army's riverside compound across from the Strand Hotel.

Left
Passengers facing to the front and rear and each sheltered by an umbrella, a rainy day sai kaa swooshes home from the market.

Top right
The Rangoon sai kaa design doesn't make sleep easy, but it's clearly possible.

Middle right
A one-armed sai kaa rider.

Bottom right
A large load of basket tops is strapped on to a sai kaa.

Sai Kaa Manufacturing

A typical sai kaa manufacturer turns vehicles out one at a time and is unlikely to make more than six a month. The starting point is an Indian Hero bicycle, which costs about $50. The teak seat and the other sidecar components are made to an absolutely standard design but are nevertheless likely to be made individually. One manufacturer showed us how he forged the metal parts himself and stamped each one with his brand name. A complete sidecar sells for about $200, although getting it licensed certainly adds to the cost.

The sidecar body with its back-to-back seat is made entirely out of inch-thick teak which is literally one inch – this teak is pre-metric. It's extremely heavy – the seat alone weighs in at 25 lbs (around 12 kg) – and also remarkably uncomfortable to ride in, but it is a beautiful piece of work. The design is completely standardized and doesn't appear to have changed in 50 years. U Hla Kyi's carpenters at the Sein Pe furniture mart make the seats as a sideline to regular furniture.

Top left
Tools in a sai kaa manufacturer's small workshop.

Middle left
Carpenter U Thein Naing works on a new sidecar body at the Sein Pe furniture workshop.

Bottom left
A roadside sai kaa repair depot on Strand Rd.

Right
Win Mun assembles a new sai kaa.

Singapore

At the southern tip of the Malay Peninsula and just over 100 km north of the equator, the city state of Singapore is Asia at its most organised, hard working and successful. That the cycle-rickshaw should survive in Singapore seems scarcely believable. Isn't this the city of air-conditioned everything? The city with the world's number one airport and home to the world's biggest fleet of Boeing 747s? Isn't this the technological center of South-East Asia where office workers ride to work on one of the world's most advanced (not to mention cleanest and safest) subway systems? And isn't the average Singaporean paypacket already ahead of its counterpart in Australia, Britain or Canada and rapidly overhauling its American equivalent? Incredibly, the cycle-rickshaw *has* survived in modern Singapore. A handful still operate as everyday transport around the markets and temples of Chinatown and Little India, and elsewhere the cycle-rickshaw has found a new role as a popular tourist attraction and symbol of the city.

Trishaw Design

Singapore's trishaw design is simplicity itself and far less specialized than the purpose-built cycle-rickshaws found in most other regions of South-East Asia (passengers in front, rider behind) or on the subcontinent (rider in front, passengers behind). The Singapore trishaw is simply a sturdy bicycle with a small sidecar bolted on to the left side. As a result it's a much more compact vehicle – the low-slung Penang trishaw is a good 50% longer overall. Don't plan on traveling two-up on a Singapore trishaw if you have more than modest hip dimensions, as the passenger seat is narrow. Surprisingly,

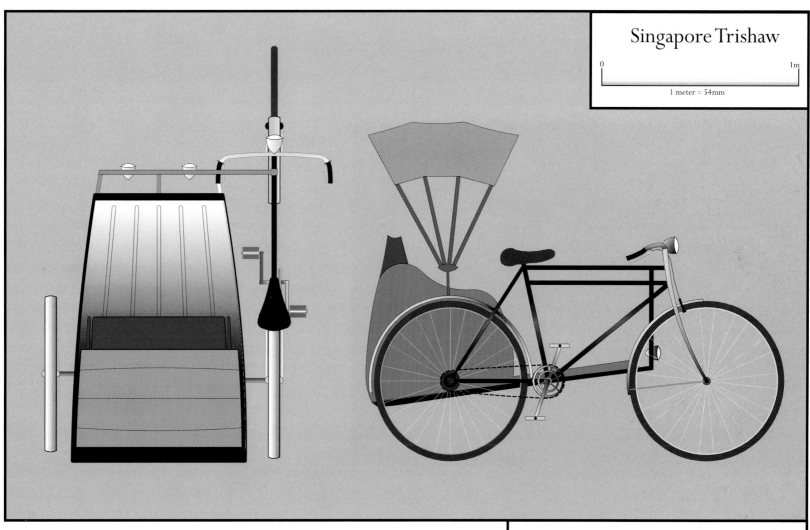

despite its compact and simple design, the Singapore trishaw is just as heavy as its counterparts in other countries.

On the road it's an easy-to-ride vehicle. Apart from steering shake, it's not difficult to maneuver or turn corners and, unlike more specialised trishaw designs with braking limited to only one end of the contraption, the Singapore trishaw has standard, albeit old-fashioned, rod-operated brakes on both the front and rear wheels of the bicycle part of the vehicle.

number of trishaws in city	300	
weight	255 lbs	116 kg
wheelbase	46 inches	116 cm
overall length	75 inches	190 cm
track	43 inches	110 cm
overall width	49 inches	125 cm
passenger seat width	25 inches	63 cm
wheel diameter	28 inches	72 cm
tire size	28 x 1.5 inches	

Singapore – How Trishaws Survive

Above
Ho Kon Bow performs a little maintenance on the well-kept Golden Lion bicycle part of his trishaw.

Right
Singapore's cycle rickshaws or trishaws have almost disappeared as everyday transport but they're enjoying a new lease of life as a tourist attraction. Here the yellow shirt convoy of trishaws takes visitors through the aromatic streets of Singapore's Little India.

Where is there room for the trishaw, as it is locally known, in a city like Singapore? Go to the market buildings in the older quarters – the Chinatown area adjoining the financial center, the Colonial District around the Raffles Hotel or Little India along Serangoon Rd – and in the mornings you will find elderly trishaw jockeys parked outside, waiting to carry shoppers and their purchases on the short trip home. The markets are now new purpose-built buildings and home is likely to be an apartment in a multi-story complex but otherwise it's a picture little changed from the early 1950s when trishaws were in their prime.

There are usually a handful of trishaws waiting to convey marketgoers home from behind the China-town Market complex on New Bridge Rd. In Little India the Zhujiao Centre at the Bras Basah Rd end of Serangoon Rd is a popular place for waiting trishaws. The Rochor Centre on Rochor Rd and Cheng Yan Court on Queen St in the Colonial District are also frequented by traditional riders.

Today, however, tourism is the more important source of a trishaw rider's income. Every night teams of riders, identified by their fluorescent yellow-green or orange T-shirts, take off on 45-minute tours of the Little India and Colonial District zones. Their passengers are predominantly Japanese package tourists, but anybody can either book a Singapore trishaw tour for about $15 per person or simply turn up at the two starting points – on Waterloo St or beside the New Bugis St development – and negotiate their own tour.

The trishaw tour riders are a mixed bunch. Certainly some of them are elderly gentlemen with colorful histories who have been pedaling the streets of Singapore for decades but others could just as easily be healthy retirees who look the part and enjoy making a little beer money in the evenings. For the younger men, trishaw riding is likely to be an after-hours second job. Some of them are college or university students, financing their studies by buying an old trishaw and joining one of the tourist teams. The opportunity to chat with tourists and to get paid for some healthy exercise is clearly part of the attraction.

Trishaws in Singapore

The hand-pulled rickshaw was banned in Singapore right after the war, in 1947, and the trishaw reigned supreme through the 1950s and 1960s, until rising prosperity and speeding traffic almost killed it off in the 1970s. A handful of trishaws have survived in the old style and can still be seen in the quiet streets and back alleys of Chinatown and Little India, taking shoppers home from the markets or delivering the goods themselves. Their riders, often wiry septuagenarians, usually look frailer than their venerable machines.

Today there are far more riders chasing the tourist dollars; like a Tour de France *peloton,* the teams of trishaw riders hurtle round the streets of Little India taking visitors on a rapid tour of the highlights. There can be as many as 50 trishaws at a time – a wonderful sight as they snake through traffic and dive off busy Serangoon Rd into the aromatic streets of this enclave of the subcontinent.

Tourist trishaws are not restricted solely to these tours; the Raffles Hotel always has a band of trishaws, waiting near the sign announcing that only cars are allowed up to the front entrance. If you want to get home from Boat Quay, Singapore's trendiest spot for drinking and dining, the queue for a taxi can stretch forever but a trishaw will pedal you away instantly – although even with stiff bargaining it will be twice the price. Further upstream, the Satay Club and Clarke Quay food and entertainment zones also have a night-time bevy of trishaw riders waiting for passengers.

Top left
A trishaw rider catches up with the news outside the Amoy St temple.

Bottom left
Yong Chee Teck in his trishaw, outside the Kuan Yin Temple on Waterloo St.

Right
Koh Chor Sang with his trishaw in Campbell Lane in Little India.

Yogyakarta

The Indonesian island of Java has a population density twice that of Japan or of the most densely populated countries of Europe, the Netherlands and England. Yogyakarta – the Y is pronounced like a J and the name is commonly abbreviated to Yogya, or Jogja – is a small fry amongst the island's mega-cities; its half a million population is dwarfed by the 10 million or so who crowd into the capital, Jakarta. The city's importance far outweighs its relatively small size, however. Yogya has always played an important role in Javanese history and was a major center in the struggle for independence from the Dutch after WW II. Furthermore it's the cultural capital of Java, an intellectual center and a center for Javanese arts and crafts. Today life in Yogya is accelerating like in every other Indonesian city but it's still a comparatively calm and quiet place where a few steps away from the main streets brings the flavor of the *kampung,* or village. It's scarcely surprising that Yogya is the number one tourist attraction of Java. It's also the country's number one city of becaks, as the cycle-rickshaws of Indonesia are known.

Becak Design

Although their design is rounded and a touch frumpy, the Yogyakarta becaks still manage to look stylish. Perhaps it's their decorative color schemes or perhaps it's simply because this is the artistic center of Indonesia. As in Hanoi and Penang, passengers ride out front in the Yogyakarta interpretation of the cycle-rickshaw. Becaks first rolled out on to Indonesian roads in the 1930s in Jakarta; at first they were looked upon as unreliable and dangerous but they soon spread right across Java and to a number of other islands in the Indonesian archipelago. Not everywhere, however; there are no becaks in Bali.

Left
A becak rider enjoys a midday snack.

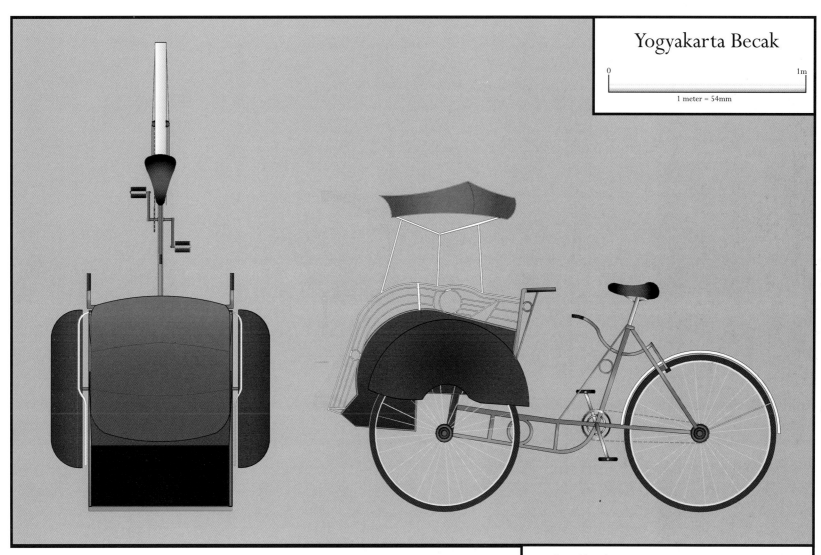

Yogyakarta Becak

0 ━━━━━━━━━━━━━━━━━━━━ 1m

1 meter = 54mm

number of becaks in city	5000	
weight	242 lbs	110 kg
wheelbase	51 inches	130 cm
overall length	91 inches	230 cm
track	35 inches	90 cm
overall width	43 inches	110 cm
passenger seat width	27 inches	69 cm
wheel diameter	28 inches	72 cm
tire size	28 x 1.5 inches	

The Disappearing Becak

The becak, the Indonesian bicycle-rickshaw, has been on retreat from Java's major cities since the early 1970s but despite motorized traffic it still flourishes in cities like Yogyakarta. In Jakarta, becaks have been on the endangered list since 1972, when they were first banned from the main streets of the capital. They were pushed back from the main boulevards and then from lesser streets around the center until late at night. Finally, when they refused to simply disappear, a vice-governor of the city announced that they were 'the last example of man exploiting man', and they were completely outlawed. Many becak riders pedaled off to more welcoming cities but thousands of becaks were seized and dumped out at sea, creating artificial reefs. The odd hardy becak may still hide out in the back blocks of Jakarta but essentially they've disappeared from the capital.

In other major cities of Java they are often banned from the major thoroughfares, but Yogyakarta is still relatively becak friendly. The city is pancake flat, so it's ideal cycle-rickshaw territory, and there's nowhere you can't get to by becak – no streets forbid them entry. Nevertheless they're seen as anachronistic and a hindrance to faster (read motorized) traffic, so officially no new becak licenses are being issued and, therefore, you can only officially buy a new rickshaw if it's to replace an old one destined for the junkyard.

Left
Decorated mudguards.

Right
A bed-carrying becak proves they're capable of bearing much larger loads than just two passengers.

This, however, is Indonesia, where 'officially' can be a very flexible concept. So between replacements of ageing machines, quiet additions to becak fleets and the odd export rickshaw, built for collectors overseas, several small factories turn out a steady trickle of brand-new becaks. Given their semi-legal status Yogyakarta's becak factories are keen to keep a low profile; but ask at the tourist office and they'll point you towards the manufacturers, and any becak pilot will know where they're made.

'Factory' is rather a big word for Yogya's becak builders; Henry Ford's assembly line has not yet reached the becak business. In fact becak building is still a cottage indus-try with construction relegated to a shed or squeezed in between general welding and machining work. They're simple, rough-and-ready vehicles, utterly lacking any high technology in their design or construction.

Becak construction is remarkably self-sufficient. The wheels, tires, saddle, bearings, pedals and sprockets are bought in but nearly everything else is made by the builders. There are two frames, the cycle frame of tubes and the framework for the seats, which is mainly welded up from flat bars. The sides of the seating area are made from teak in order to survive a tough life outside in sun and rain. The red vinyl padded seat is made on the spot and bamboo framing is built around the folding frame-work for the hood, which is stitched up on an elderly sewing machine. Then a few coats of paint are slapped on the frames by hand, the wheels are attached and, as a finale, the brightly painted mudguards are bolted in place.

Above
Resplendent with their polished teak, shiny vinyl and bright red paint, a batch of new becaks await delivery.

Left
Becak rear wheel assemblies and bamboo hood bows.

Licensed and plated, the shiny new becak is ready to hit the streets of Yogyakarta (or head off overseas) once $300 has changed hands. Foreigners and becak fleet owners will probably be paying cash, but local owner-operators may well opt for a time-payment plan. Simply hand over about $5 a week and in less than two years, the becak's yours.

Yogyakarta's small-scale becak factories turn out from two or three up to 12 to 15 becaks a week, depending on demand. Spend a few days riding the becaks and you may start to pick up subtle design differences from one constructor to another. Athough the frames and major components are essentially identical (and nearly every becak seems to boast a Five Rams saddle) there are minor giveaway differences in design. One type has horizontal slats under the seat, for example; another has vertical bars. Remark-ably there's little attempt to individualize the paintwork – a standard 'two volcanoes, a lake and some trees' design goes on most mudguards. Others are simply painted a single color, a few have leaping tigers, one or two display advertising for local hotels and there's a small fleet promoting the local McDonalds, but the exotic one-off becak is unusual and a really colorful fleet design doesn't seem to exist.

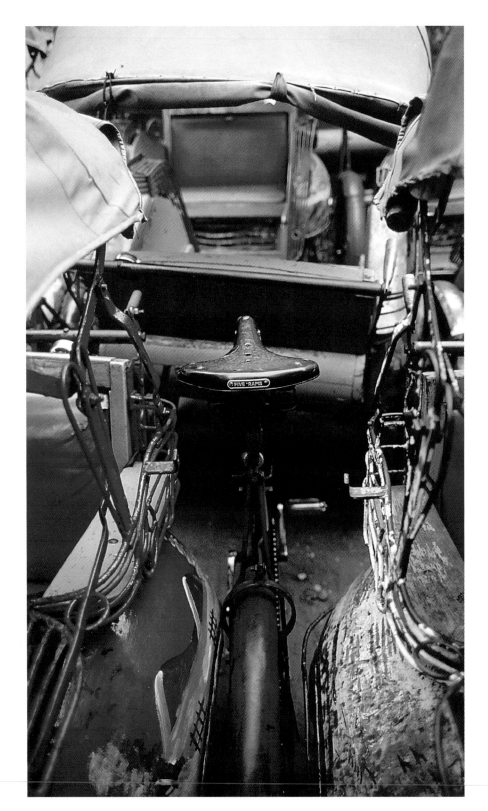

Right
A becak assembler fits crank bearings to a new frame while behind him a recently completed becak awaits delivery.

Becak Fleets

There are few becak owner-operators. Most of Yogya's 5000 becaks are owned in fleets and rented out to their riders, the *tukang becak*, by the day. Riders typically pay about 30 cents for either the morning to late afternoon day shift or the evening and night shift. Becaks with names like Dwi Tunggal, Pasti Jaya, ABC, Gendingan, Makar Jaya or Ningsih are the three-wheeled equivalents of Yellow Cabs, Silver Tops or Checker Cabs in the West. Down a narrow alleyway off busy Jalan Parangtritis, near the popular Jalan Prawirotaman tourist enclave and the equally busy Pasar Prawirotaman morning market, are four *pos becak,* the home bases for becak fleets.

Left
A becak maintenance man keeps watch on a Jalan Parangtritis becak fleet.

Right
At the end of the day shift the Rewalu becak fleet is marshaled in the yard for the night.

Above
Yosephin Sudarini, book-keeper at the Rewalu becak
headquarters, checks in the riders at the end of their
shift.

Between 6 and 8 am fleet owner Eatot Subroto is simultaneously bringing in the last of the night shift becaks and sending them out with their day riders. Eatot started 24 years ago with one becak and gradually built up his fleet to today's roster of 40-odd becaks, all emblazoned with the name Gaya on each side. Gaya is his eight-year-old daughter, heiress to a becak fleet already named after her. On Jalan Prawirotaman itself a smaller fleet of becaks operates from right in the street.

The day shift ends between 3 and 5 pm. As the Rewalu fleet's 90-odd becaks wend their way home, on the other side of town, we're waiting for them to arrive. Yosephin Sudarini checks in each becak on her large ledger and collects the rental fee from each rider. There's some servicing and cleaning going on before the becaks are packed away into a courtyard for the night. Although the books seem to indicate that Rewalu only rent out about three-quarters of its fleet each day, there's an absolutely brand-new becak waiting in the courtyard, looking like it's not yet had its first day on the road.

Top
A becak owner at the Jalan Prawirotaman becak center; behind him is the roll call of riders.

Bottom
Becak fleet owner Eatot Subroto.

Left
The Rewalu becak compound even has a small kitchen where drinks and meals are prepared for the riders.

Top right
On Jalan Malioboro, resting becak riders play cards.

Bottom right
Becaks return to the Rewalu compound at the end of the afternoon shift.

Sugiyono's Multinational Becak

'Sur, je parle français' is painted across the back of Sugiyono's pastel-painted becak. 'Multinational' is written down one side at the front and a row of flags appears down the other. Sugiyono, who is very proud that for several years his name appeared in the French *Guide du Routard* guidebook to Indonesia, has been a becak rider for 26 years. His father was killed in the independence struggle with the Dutch, right after WW II. Despite Sugiyono's education (he speaks fluent English and French), finding work in Yogya is difficult. A Dutch friend sent him the money to buy this becak, but a few years ago Sugiyono's daughter caught dengue fever and he had to sell the vehicle to pay for her hospital treatment. Today he rents it from a fleet owner, but his beautiful machine is permanently reserved for his use and he rides it back to his kampung, six km south of central Yogya, at the end of each day. Every couple of years Sugiyono repaints the becak in a new but equally vivid color scheme. He has two daughters, both in high school, two sons who work in an ice cream factory at Bogor and an eldest son at home, still trying to find a job.

Above
Indonesian becaks are squat, heavy-looking and crude
in their construction but also colorful.

Ride a Becak

After only a few turns of the pedals down a *gang*, the Indonesian word for a small back alley, with my becak's regular operator warning me to go *'pelan, pelan'* (slowly, slowly), it's quickly obvious why becak riders lope along with such lazy ease – moving fast would be terrifying. My becak feels horribly unstable. There's none of that natural two-wheeler, 'hands off' stability; in fact the front of the thing feels as if it would like to flop over to one side at any instant.

Nor does it take corners with any ease. I have to force it into the bend and muscle it straight again as I come out. I can't lean into the corner and then, on the exit from the corner, let my becak bring itself back to the vertical, as I would with a motorcycle or bicycle. Nor is there the self-centering steering effect car drivers are used to. At the first acute corner I come to I collide, fortunately gently, with the wall because I simply haven't yanked my becak back hard enough.

Top
Becak rider waits outside the Beringharjo Market.

Bottom
Becak riders sometimes sit behind the saddle – it makes it easier to chat with their passengers.

Stopping is clearly not a becak's forte either. The single brake on the rear wheel is a crude affair applied by pushing a lever down between the rider's legs. Gentle braking can be achieved by simply pulling back on the pedals; there's no freewheel so if the becak is moving the pedals must be moving too. I make a mental note not to lounge back so nonchalantly as becak riders push me towards oncoming traffic in future. Since my collision with the wall my becak's usual pilot hasn't been riding quite so nonchalantly either – after his initial *pelan, pelan* instructions sank in he took up the unusual, for him, position at the front. Nevertheless he reclines back in the seat and waves lazily to his fellow riders. They watch with amusement as we return down my hotel street, with the tourist doing the sweaty hard work for once.

Left
The rickshaw at its best; two ladies ride home from market in a Yogyakarta becak.

Right
A becak rider outside the Jalan Prawirotaman Market.

Rickshaws

A Short History of the Rickshaw

The rickshaw was invented in around 1870. In fact the invention of the *jinrikisha,* or 'human-powered vehicle', was one of the first examples of Japanese technological ingenuity, a clear predecessor to CD players, video recorders and Honda motorcycles. It was also a wonderful example of the irresistible power of technological change, an invention which not only gave you more but cost you less.

Back in that unmotorized age you could always walk, of course, but otherwise personal transport in a city context meant one of two things. If you could afford the animals, the feed, the space and the associated staff you could have a horse and carriage. If that was too expensive or too inconvenient you could have a sedan chair or palanquin. A sedan chair didn't take up too much space but did require two men on call, to carry you from place to place. The invention of the jinrikisha was an example of blindingly obvious thinking: fire the man carrying the back of the sedan chair and replace him with two wheels. In one stroke you had not only halved the labor force, you had also dramatically increased the speed, for one man pulling a jinrikisha could travel much faster than two men carrying a sedan chair.

The staid and upright becak of Yogyakarta.

It was no wonder this Japanese invention caught on so rapidly. Within a few years the rickshaw, as the name was anglicized, swept across Asia. Rickshaws and their pullers became a familiar sight in cities across Japan and China, throughout South-East Asia and across the length and breadth of the Indian subcontinent. At first they were strictly private transport; a family would own a rickshaw and employ their personal rickshaw puller to take them where they wished. Soon, however, the rickshaw progressed from private to public transport. While buses, trains and tramways became popular means of mass public transport, the rickshaw became the unchallenged form of small-scale public transport and remained that way until the taxi came along.

To be absolutely correct, the rickshaw did not really originate in Japan. There are illustrations of crude wheeled versions of a sedan chair in use in Europe up to 200 years earlier. The French *chaise roulante,* or mobile chair, was undoubtedly in use during the reign of Louis XIV (1638–1715) but this contraption was propeled by two men, one in front, one behind, and never became popular. Although the idea of the rickshaw was clearly conceived much earlier than its Asian birthdate, the rickshaw did not become a success at that time for a simple reason: the necessary technology did not exist. Smoother road surfaces, rubber for the wheels and steel for the vehicle's construction were required before the rickshaw finally became feasible. Why did the rickshaw never find a home in Europe? Probably because it was invented too late. By the time the rickshaw was technically feasible the cities of Europe were already endowed with extensive railway and tramway systems and the general population had reached a level of affluence that did not cater for large numbers of low-paid rickshaw pullers.

Even the jinrikisha may not have been invented by a Japanese. Five contenders have been lined up to claim the credit but the name that most frequently tops the list is Jonathan Gable, an American missionary who, so it is claimed, devised the rickshaw for his frail wife.

The rickshaw's origins may be unclear but its subsequent spread is well documented. By 1880, only 10 years after its first appearance, there were over 150,000 in Japan; the clever device had even enjoyed the highest seal of approval when the Emperor Meiji used one to travel around his capital. In 1872, however, the Tokyo authorities had already had to regulate the rickshaw trade, banning the risqué paintings which appeared on their rear panels and stipulating that rickshaw pullers should, at the very least, wear something more discrete than a loincloth. Already rickshaws were starting to appear in Chinese cities in the region, including Hong Kong, Shanghai and Singapore. By 1890 Japan's rickshaw numbers had peaked at around 200,000, of which about 50,000 were in Tokyo, and the sedan chair had been driven to extinction. They had become a major export, and although there were fledgling local industries in other countries, the Japanese machines were always assumed to be the best. By the turn of the century rickshaws were in use not only across China but down through French Indochina, into British-governed Malaya and Burma, and then right across India. Rickshaws had even spread to South Africa (where their bicycle offspring, the cycle-rickshaw, can still be found in Durban) and the odd example had popped up in Australia and the Americas.

With the new century rickshaw numbers began to fall in Japan, but in other parts of Asia they were still riding an upward curve. By this time Beijing had nearly as many rickshaws as Tokyo in its prime, and lesser cities like Singapore and Shanghai could also boast over 10,000 of the infernal machines. Infernal because almost from the start city authorities harbored an intense dislike of rickshaws, an opprobrium which was eventually transferred to the cycle-rickshaw and in some places continues to this day.

The rickshaw's history in Singapore exemplified the official antagonism they engendered. The rickshaw took about 10 years to find its way from its Japanese birthplace to Singapore, by way of Shanghai. It was an immediate hit. The Singapore rickshaw population numbered over 1000 in 1880, the year the first example arrived, and the city's *gharry* (two-wheel horse carriage) drivers were soon on strike, demanding that rickshaws should be used strictly as a private means of transport. The gharry drivers' protests were insightful but useless; by the turn of the century the rickshaw had pushed the horse carriage to the edge of extinction.

Nevertheless rickshaws were far from popular with the city authorities and attempts were made to restrict their numbers to 2500. However, city hall's efforts to stand in the rickshaws' way were no more successful than those of the gharry drivers and when, in 1892, the limit on numbers was abandoned, the city's rickshaw population immediately quadrupled. Singapore had clearly been sheltering a huge fleet of illegal, unlicensed vehicles. Even with many more licensed rickshaws, a huge number of unlicensed ones continued to operate; in 1910 estimates put the city's rickshaw battalions at 20,000, half of them unlicensed.

In turn-of-the-century Singapore a pattern of rickshaw ownership and use had already been established which continues to this day in other parts of Asia. Only a minuscule 2% or less of the impoverished rickshaw pullers owned their rickshaws. Most vehicles were marshaled in small fleets of up to 20, although some big-time owners had 50 or even 100 rickshaws. Typically, a puller had to hand over a quarter of his earnings to rent his vehicle, leaving barely enough cash to survive and certainly not enough to put towards buying his own rickshaw.

The Singapore government did little to make life easier for the hard-working pullers. A thicket of bureaucracy, tangled with the inevitable miscommunications between the often illiterate Chinese-speaking pullers and the English-speaking authorities, compounded the problems. For 32 years, from 1892 to 1924, a Mr Hooper, backed by a team of 60 Malay clerical workers, ruled the Rickshaw Department, enforcing the city's Rickshaw

A cyclo rolls by the Municipal Theater in Hanoi.

Ordinances with an iron hand. In 1896, 5277 rickshaws were seized because their pullers were inappropriately clothed! A year later, 311 vehicles were hauled off the road because their pullers appeared 'tired' or 'unfit'. On average a rickshaw was likely to be impounded four times a year. The reasons for the confiscations were often a mystery to the rickshaw pullers and payments of bribes to city rickshaw officials were commonplace. In 1897 the pullers' simmering anger led to a four-day rickshaw strike that almost brought the city to a halt and was only terminated by the dual effects of martial law and Chinese New Year.

Rickshaw pullers were accused of blocking traffic, failing to pick up and put down passengers at the designated rickshaw stands, loitering around looking for fares and generally being a confounded nuisance. The fact that rickshaw owners were punished, by having their rickshaws impounded, for offences committed by the rickshaw pullers added to the turmoil. When the governor's horse carriage collided with a rickshaw in 1901, the ongoing dispute between rickshaw owners and pullers on one side and the city authorities on the other again threatened to boil over, with the governor's unilateral decision to crack down on rickshaws leading to Singapore's second rickshaw strike. This time the strike was broken when the government threatened to deport certain important rickshaw owners. The only tangible result of this clash was that the Rickshaw Department now began to prosecute pullers as well as owners. The sole serious attempt to ease the rickshaw pullers' lot was an ordinance passed shortly before WW I which reduced the maximum seat width by 3½ inches to 24 inches (about 60 cm) so that a rickshaw could only carry one passenger. In fact the poor pullers still ended up hauling two people around; passengers were simply squeezed into a smaller space. Remarkably Singapore's cycle-rickshaws still have a seat width of about 24 inches.

Finally, in the 1920s, the authorities decided to get tough with rickshaws, first by refusing to issue new licenses and then by imposing an annual 15% reduction in their numbers. Pious explanations were offered about the inhumanity of the industry, but the real reason was probably the motor car. By this time Singapore had lots of them; their affluent owners wielded considerable power and rickshaws got in their way. Growing numbers of small buses and fleets of taxis also began to make the rickshaw less and less attractive. At the same time bicycles began to throng the streets and the trishaw or cycle-rickshaw made its Singapore debut. By 1935 there were already more trishaws than rickshaws and by the time the war swept across the region the hand-pulled rickshaw was clearly in terminal decline. From the late

1920s to the late 1930s the city's rickshaw population of 10,000 had fallen by two-thirds.

Further north up the Malay peninsula in Penang the rickshaw had an equally difficult time. The first jinrikisha was already in use in Penang in the late 1800s and by 1903 their numbers had peaked at 3696 publicly licensed rickshaws. There were still 2000 in use in 1940, just before the Japanese occupation. There were also privately owned jinrikishas, for a Chinese merchant or tradesman might keep his own rickshaw and rickshaw puller. Their numbers peaked at 678 in 1912 and declined rapidly after cars became more common, from the mid-1920s.

Jinrikishas were always a problem to the city administration. In 1907 Alan W B Hamilton, the Registrar of Jinrikishas & Hackney Carriages, noted that:

> There is a marked improvement in the way pullers now observe the rules of the road. Perfection is still very far off and will I am afraid never be attained, when every Chinese coolie who is temporarily out of employment takes to pulling a jinrikisha in the meantime.
>
> On the occasion of the visit of HRH the Duke of Connaught to Penang, sixteen rubber tyred jinrikishas were provided with special pullers for the conveyance of the royal party at night from the Residency to Swettenham Wharf on their departure. The journey was completed in under seventeen minutes …

In 1908 the registrar had no less than 1677 cases of jinrikisha malfeasance to deal with. He obtained 977 convictions for 'obstructing traffic', 70 for 'demanding more than the authorised fare' or other forms of 'disorderly behaviour' and 69 for 'carrying bulky and other prohibited articles'. He also had to handle offenses against rickshaw pullers, including cases of refusal to pay the fare, damaging a rickshaw or even assaulting the rickshaw puller. In 1929, George Bilainkin, editor of the *Straits Echo*, wrote of his first rickshaw experience in Penang:

> Suddenly I seemed to be a prisoner, surrounded by no fewer than a dozen little carriages, not unlike the bath chairs in the parks of Bath or Kensington Gardens. In front of the place for the passenger, who must sit high up, between two enormous wheels with rubber tyres, were the shafts. Inside there stood the Chinese … They were jostling and pushing each other out of the way … I walked slowly through the smell of old shirts and shouting humanity to the oldest coolie who now stood away at the back of the group … The old man almost doubled himself up between the shafts, turned the carriage to the right and to the left, looked back to see whether there was any traffic behind, and was off.
>
> The master was on the throne. The slave was in harness.

Rickshaws had a colorful history in Singapore and Penang, but nowhere was the rickshaw's influence so important or its story so violently dramatic as in

Rickshaws are repaired and restored in this Calcutta workshop.

Beijing. The first Japanese rickshaws had rolled on to Beijing's streets in 1886 but the city's mule cart drivers, clearly perceiving the threat to their trade, hurled them into a canal. Rickshaws reappeared in 1900 and although their return coincided with the Boxer Rebellion, when all foreign-manufactured goods were suspect, they quickly caught on. By the mid-1920s the old mule carts had disappeared and Beijing's population of less than a million was hauled around by 60,000 rickshaw pullers. It was estimated that one in every five people in the city depended on the rickshaw for their livelihood. The rickshaw was the city's most popular form of both public and private transport and for a time rickshaw pullers made a surprisingly respectable living.

As rickshaw numbers in Beijing continued to grow and the country as a whole became increasingly chaotic, the rickshaw pullers' living standards declined disastrously. In Lao She's book *Rickshaw*, the hero, 'Camel' Xiangzi, follows a desperate downhill path mirrored by the Vietnamese cycle-rickshaw rider in the recent film *Cyclo*. In Tokyo rickshaw numbers began to fall as soon as electric tramways appeared in 1903. Twenty years later, when the first streetcars arrived in Beijing, the pattern was repeated. Beijing's mule drivers had opposed the introduction of the rickshaw and now it was the rickshaw pullers' turn to lie down in the tracks of progress. Government suggestions that rickshaw pullers would be given preferential consideration for tramway jobs defused the protests but the promises came to nothing, of course.

It took just six months for the new-fangled transport system to sideline a third of Beijing's rickshaws, but once the initial tramway enthusiasm had worn off rickshaws bounded back and by the late 1920s the city had 30,000 registered rickshaws. The rickshaw pullers had formed a union demanding all sorts of restrictions on the city's buses and streetcars, and in October 1929 the dispute erupted into violence, with 25,000 rickshaw workers battling with bus and streetcar employees and tipping over 60 of the city's 90 streetcars. Mass arrests, and the firing squad for three key union leaders, ended the struggle, but in fact it was WW II and the arrival of the cycle-rickshaw, not streetcars and buses, which finally destroyed the Beijing rickshaw.

In many cities across south and east Asia the golden age of the rickshaw was probably the early years of the 20th century, a period when they were challenged by tramway and railway competition but taxis and buses had not yet become ubiquitous. Throughout the region rickshaw numbers started to decline during the 1920s and 1930s but they were still an enormously popular means of transport right up until WW II.

Jonathan Gable may have invented the rickshaw but it was the Japanese who really popularized it; the switch to cycle-rickshaws also owes much to Japan. It may not have been the Japanese who actually dreamed up the idea of melding a bicycle with a rickshaw to create the cycle-rickshaw, but it certainly was Pearl Harbor and the Pacific theater of WW II which led to the cycle-rickshaw's popularity. Starved of fuel, taxis and buses were soon stationary in many Asian cities and some alternative form of transport, something faster than a hand-pulled rickshaw, was desperately needed. The cycle-rickshaw, which 10 years earlier might have been seen simply as a last-ditch effort to prolong the rickshaw's life, and which was already facing the same official disapproval as the rickshaw, suddenly became the perfect means of transport.

In Singapore it's theorized that the cycle-rickshaw was the product of local Chinese ingenuity heroically coping with the wartime fuel shortages. In fact cycle-rickshaws were in use in Singapore well before WW II and the city always had a pioneering attitude towards bicycle-powered vehicles. The Upton Park tricycle, an early rickshawlike device wedded to a chainless penny-farthing style bicycle, was actually advertized in Singapore newspapers in 1886, although it's unclear if any actually appeared on the streets. In 1914, 15 'pedal rickshaw' licenses were taken out, and this time some of them did actually make it into use, although only for a few weeks.

Cycle-rickshaws made their real appearance in the late 1920s and Singapore soon became the leading cycle-rickshaw city. By the start of WW II their numbers were approaching 10,000. Gordon Ang, a 67-year-old bus driver, vividly recalls pedaling trishaws around Singapore as a teenager in 1943 and 1944. He scoffed at the idea that they were invented by the Japanese occupying force.

'There was no petrol so there were no taxis,' he said. 'We had to have some means of transport.'

Some Singapore historic sources even pinpoint the trishaw's inventor – a Mr Sunny Tan who lived on Balestier Rd. Elderly trishaw riders can be equally emphatic that the trishaw was a local invention, during 'Germany time'.

In other cities the cycle-rickshaw had also made a tentative appearance before the war, then established itself strongly during the war years. It appeared in Indian cities, including Calcutta and Dhaka, during the 1930s while the unusual *becak* of Indonesia, in which the passengers ride precariously out front, was first seen on the streets of Jakarta in 1936. At the start becaks were notoriously unstable, as well as unpopular with other road users, but they soon caught on. After the war their numbers exploded: 25,000 becaks circulated on Jakarta's streets in the early 1950s, growing to well over 100,000 by 1970. They were first restricted in the city center in 1972 and then banned. Between 1980 and 1985 city authorities seized 50,000 becaks and dumped them in the sea.

By the end of WW II the cycle-rickshaw had become a familiar sight in cities across the region and the old hand-pulled rickshaw was rapidly heading towards extinction. Singapore banned them completely in 1947; Tokyo still had 400 in 1950 but four years later they were all gone. The last handful rolled on into the 1960s in Penang, while in Madras, in India, the state government finally got rid of the last 1300 old rickshaws in 1973 by the simple expedient of replacing the lot with free cycle-rickshaws.

In some cities, like Singapore, the cycle-rickshaw enjoyed a brief heyday through the 1950s and into the 1960s before increasing prosperity and speeding traffic drove it off the roads. In Beijing Communist distaste for such a tangible symbol of personal exploitation may have reduced cycle-rickshaw numbers, but some sources insist that they were finally driven off the roads in 1972 in order to clean things up for a visit by that prime capitalist, Richard Nixon. Although the cycle-rickshaw had not appeared in Japan prior to WW II, it did make a brief appearance in the straitened days after the war. It's estimated that Tokyo had 4000 *rintaku* or pedicabs in 1947 and a handful survived into the late 1950s. The Singapore pattern of rapid growth and slow decline has been repeated, albeit at a slower pace, in Penang (Malaysia), Manila (Philippines) and, at this very moment, in Yogyakarta (Indonesia). In Hanoi (Vietnam) greater events, in the form of the Vietnam War, have given the cycle-rickshaw a much longer life but even there faster traffic is killing it off. In Dhaka (Bangladesh), however, the cycle-rickshaw is still dominant, pushing all other forms of transport, public and private, to the sidelines and continuing to increase in numbers despite frantic government efforts to curb the growth. And in one city, Calcutta (India), the cycle-rickshaw's predecessor, the old hand-pulled rickshaw, still survives.

Gloves, drinks – winter equipment for a Beijing tricycle.

Cycle-Rickshaw Design & Manufacturing

Why did it take so long for the rickshaw to commence its seemingly inevitable romance with the bicycle to produce their equally inevitable offspring, the cycle-rickshaw? And why hasn't that inevitable offspring gone on developing, mutating, progressing and refining to eventually produce some kind of super cycle-rickshaw? Instead, the cycle-rickshaw popped up in a number of different forms in a number of different places, all at around the same time, and then simply came to a halt. There does not appear to have been any cross-fertilization of design ideas: in each rickshaw city, cycle-rickshaw design seems to take a different form. Nor does there appear to be any continuing design development;

in every rickshaw city, the cycle-rickshaw remains unchanged from its original ancestor of 50 or more years ago.

This combination of isolated development and stagnant design can be put down to several factors. Colonialism may have played a part in the totally separate strands of cycle-rickshaw design. Prior to WW II there was remarkably little trade between, say, the French colony of Vietnam, the British colonies of Burma and Malaya or the Dutch colony of Indonesia. So each country's original interpretation of the cycle-rickshaw was unlikely to have much influence on cycle-rickshaw design in one of its neighbors. The arrival of WW II in the region may have established the cycle-rickshaw's importance in the transport picture but at the same time it increased the isolation of individual countries.

The relatively small scale of cycle-rickshaw production combined with its essentially simple design also kept manufacturing down at the cottage-industry end of the engineering spectrum. In some countries, like Bangladesh or Burma, making cycle-rickshaws is simply an assembly operation, a matter of putting together a mélange of bicycle parts and a limited number of pure rickshaw components; since no manufacturer ever makes very many cycle-rickshaws there is no impetus to produce an improved design. In other countries, like Indonesia or Vietnam, cycle-rickshaw design is more specialized but the quantities made are still too small to encourage development and progress.

The sad fact is that despite their initial appearance of engineering simplicity and purity, all the Asian cycle-rickshaws are rather horrible examples of design.

A rickshaw traffic jam in the crowded alleyways of Old Dhaka.

For a start they're ridiculously heavy. A modern mountain bike weighs less than 30 lbs (13.5 kg), so why should a cycle-rickshaw weigh six or eight times as much? Even before the passengers climb on, the poor rickshaw rider may have over 200 lbs (90 kg) of machine to pedal around. With rider and passengers on board, a rickshaw can easily weigh over 600 lbs (270 kg), four or five times as much as a normal bicycle and rider. Yet many rickshaw designs have only one brake – a regular, old-fashioned, lever-operated brake on the front wheel of an Agra or Dhaka cycle-rickshaw, or an awkward form of foot or hand-operated brake on the rear wheel of a Yogyakarta, Penang or Hanoi machine. Hardly surprisingly, cycle-rickshaws don't stop very well – so it's just as well they rarely go very fast!

Getting up speed is made still more difficult by the lack of gearing on most rickshaws; only Macau and Beijing cycle-rickshaws have any kind of gearing system. The Macau version has a complicated but remarkably effective two-speed gearing system and the Beijing machine has a very primitive derailleur gearing system which requires stopping and manually changing the chain from one sprocket to another to take full advantage of the gearing possibilities! There has been little attempt to adapt bicycle gearing systems to cycle-rickshaw use, although in most cases bicycle components would not be strong enough any way. Another example of compromised design is found on the Agra or Dhaka machines; only one of their twin rear wheels is driven because they have no differential system which would allow the wheels to go at different speeds around corners.

For all their weight, many of the cycle-rickshaw designs have remarkably low rigidity – a combination of poor design and the compromises inevitable when trying to adapt bicycle components to an entirely different use. The Agra and Dhaka cycle-rickshaws basically link the front half of a regular bicycle to a rear subframe which carries the passenger seats and rear axle; the bits and pieces used to link these two assemblies are heavy, primitive and not very effective. As a result the whole contraption wriggles around and often feels extremely unstable. When it comes to the sidecar-style cycle-rickshaws, the Singapore and Manila versions are at least fairly rigidly bolted together – but the Rangoon one, where blocks of wood are used to attach the sidecar to the bicycle frame, is hopeless. Rangoon riders must sometimes feel as if the cycle and sidecar are about to shoot off in totally different directions.

If the meeting point between bicycle and rickshaw presents one set of difficulties, the sheer unsuitability of bicycle components for cycle-rickshaw use is quite another problem. Many bicycle components are not strong or substantial enough for the heavy-duty demands of a cycle-rickshaw, while others are simply unsuitable. Bicycle forks, for example, have 'trail', the distance between where the pivoting axis of the front forks intersects the ground and the contact point of the front wheel. Trail is what gives a bicycle its natural tendency to turn a corner when leaned to the right or left and to go straight ahead when the bicycle is upright. Trail is pointless on a cycle-rickshaw, which does not tilt when cornering, and in fact having front forks with trail designed for a bicycle actually makes the cycle-rickshaw less stable.

So if someone made a better rickshaw would the world beat a path to the clever manufacturer's front door? There have been attempts to make a better rickshaw, not always with great success. In the 1970s an Oxford University and Oxfam project produced the Oxtrike, a rickshaw design which included a differential for the rear axle, three-speed gears and braking on the rear axle. Over 100 Oxtrikes were produced and sent for evaluation to a number of developing countries, but they never caught on. Some of the Oxtrike ideas were incorporated in a new rickshaw design developed in 1978–80 at BUET, the

Bangladesh University of Engineering & Technology. To make it more suitable for manufacturing in Bangladesh, more local components were used and a locally manufactured gear system was devised. The BUET cycle-rickshaw failed because it was not a significant improvement over current designs: it was heavier, more expensive to make and the gears did not work very well. The project was eventually superseded by the equally unsuccessful Mishuk project to develop a motorized cycle-rickshaw.

With its huge cycle-rickshaw fleet, Bangladesh would seem to be the ideal place to build a better rickshaw, but even spending half a million dollars in the 1980s on the Canadian-funded Inter Pares project failed to put a better rickshaw on the market. This project developed a rickshaw which was 10% lighter and yet much stronger than the standard Bangladeshi machines; it was also much easier to steer and had far more powerful brakes. On the other hand, the new rickshaw's suspension system was no improvement over the current model; its two-speed gears never worked properly and it was just as unstable. In the end fewer than 200 of these new rickshaws were produced before interest faded away.

In recent years a number of Western manufacturers have attempted to build modern cycle-rickshaws, usually for tourist use in the West. Today you can find modern cycle-rickshaws in cities as widely separated as Oxford (England), San Diego and San Francisco (USA) and Berlin (Germany). Generally these Western cycle-rickshaws adapt mountain bike components to cycle-rickshaw use, but they do boast rigid one-piece frames, differentials so both rear wheels are driven, brakes to the front and rear wheels (hydraulic disk brakes on some of the machines) and modern gearing. Unfortunately they're still as heavy as ever and they're also much more expensive. For all its imperfections you can buy a shiny new cycle-rickshaw for $300 to $400 in Dhaka, Rangoon or Yogyakarta. Count on 10 times as much to buy a new one in the West.

Riding Rickshaws

At some time during our visits to each cycle-rickshaw city I jumped on board and went for a test ride. Surprisingly it was not as hard work at it looks, for despite their hefty weight cycle-rickshaws are generally pretty low geared and as long as the streets are flat it doesn't take a great effort to roll them along. In Rob Gallagher's exhaustive study of the rickshaw business, *The Rickshaws of Bangladesh*, he concludes that although rickshaw riding is hard work it's not any more arduous than other manual activities, like farming. What I found much more difficult than merely going forward was steering and stopping.

Pushing a Dhaka rickshaw through a monsoon flood.

Cycle-rickshaws do not have a bicycle's natural stability. Taking a corner on a bicycle is a simple matter of leaning slightly into the curve; when you straighten up, the bicycle does as well. That certainly isn't the case with a cycle-rickshaw, which has to be wrestled into the corner and hauled back out of it. My first rickshaw experience, on a Yogyakarta becak, included a brush with a wall because I did not use enough brute force to straighten the beast out as we exited a corner. Riding a rickshaw in Agra, I had quite the opposite experience. The subcontinent's rickshaws use a normal bicycle front fork and wheel, and as a result the front half of a rickshaw wants to act like a bicycle and veer off to one side when a sideways force is applied. I was cruising along a quiet road in the Agra cantonment district when a minor bump in the road suddenly sent my rickshaw diving off the road, skittering across the grass and plunging into the bushes!

Even without steering problems, the lack of rigidity which many cycle-rickshaws suffer from makes riding a less than straightforward activity. Most cycle-rickshaws are a mix of bicycle and rickshaw parts, joined together with a distinct deficiency of engineer-ing precision. The front and back halves often feel as if they're squirming around and intent on disappearing in totally different directions. The Agra and Rangoon versions were particularly lacking in rigidity and disconcerting to ride.

Having got your rickshaw moving and round the odd corner, the final problem is bringing it to a halt. Cycle-rickshaws have lousy brakes. In most cases the problem of designing brakes for both ends seems to have been too much for the rickshaw's designer, who's opted to make do with braking at one end only. As a result a weighty rickshaw with three people aboard has less braking power than a bicycle. The passengers-to-the-rear cycle-rickshaws of Agra and Dhaka have a regular bicycle front brake, although it is operated by both front brake levers in tandem so at least you can squeeze it twice as hard. The passengers-to-the-front cycle-rickshaws of Hanoi, Penang and Yogya have different forms of brake on the rear wheel only. The Penang and Hanoi versions are operated by a foot pedal which allows the rider to stand his weight on the brakes but requires an awkward motion when taking his feet off the pedals. All three are remarkably crude in their operation, and the Hanoi rickshaw not only provides minimal braking but makes horrible noises into the bargain. None of them stop very well.

Books & Films

Anyone intent on learning more about rickshaws and cycle-rickshaws should start their search with Rob Gallagher's *The Rickshaws of Bangladesh* (University Press, Dhaka, 1992). This exhaustive 700-page study of the rickshaw business in Bangladesh actually extends its horizons far wider, taking in the whole story of the development and spread of the rickshaw from its birth in Japan. The hand-pulled rickshaw story is followed by the creation of the cycle-rickshaw and its varied success in many countries of Asia. The use of three-wheeled bicycles for transporting both freight and passengers in Central America, Africa and elsewhere is also studied.

In Bangladesh the book investigates the rickshaw's important position in the country's transport system and castigates the government for its unimaginative treatment of this huge industry. There are chapters devoted to rickshaw design (and lack of design) and to the surprisingly unsuccessful efforts from various quarters to 'build a better rickshaw'. The human side is covered with a look at the working lives of rickshaw riders, rickshaw owners, rickshaw builders, rickshaw mechanics and even rickshaw artists.

A French metal model of a Vietnamese cyclo.

The rickshaw has clearly been a key component in the transport story for many Asian cities but on numerous occasions it has influenced much more. It's hard to ignore a business that directly or indirectly employs one in every five people in a major city, as the rickshaw business did in Beijing earlier this century. Similarly the rickshaw strikes in Singapore around the turn of the century terrified the colonial city's government not because of the transport turmoil that resulted, but because they revealed how many men the rickshaw industry could mobilize on the street. In Jakarta in the 1970s anti-government protests were often led by disgruntled becak riders. In Dhaka today the rickshaw business employs a huge percentage of the city's workforce, despite the government's efforts to sideline the industry.

A Nepalese painted wooden model of a subcontinent rickshaw.

Historical and sociological studies in which the rickshaw and its workers play a key role include *Rickshaw Coolie: A People's History of Singapore, 1880–1940* by James Francis Warren (Oxford University Press, 1986), *Rickshaw Beijing: City People & Politics in the 1920s* by David Strand (University of California Press, 1993) and *Calcutta Cycle-Rickshaw Pullers: A Sociological Study* by Subir Bandyopadhyay (South Asia Books, 1990). Transport economists have also turned their attention to the rickshaw in books like *Rikisha to Rapid Transit: Urban Public Transport Systems & Policy in Southeast Asia* by Peter J Rimmer (Australian National University Press, 1986). Michael Wise's *Travellers' Tales of Old Singapore* (Times Books International, 1996) has several fascinating historical accounts of encounters with rickshaws, including a distinctly one-sided view of the 1901 rickshaw strike.

The rickshaw and cycle-rickshaw have certainly played their part in fiction, most notably in books about Calcutta and Jakarta. Dominique Lapierre's *The City of Joy* (Arrow Books, 1986) follows the life of hard-working Hasari Pal, the 'human horse' who is driven to east India's dark metropolis by rural poverty and struggles to survive as a lowly rickshaw-wallah.

Indonesian becaks are always in the background of *The Year of Living Dangerously* (Thomas Nelson, 1978), Christopher J Koch's book about journalists in Jakarta during 1965, the confusing and tumultuous year that ended Sukarno's period as the head of Indonesia. A journalists' becak race around the huge traffic circle in front of the Indonesia Hotel is one of the book's memorable rickshaw moments.

Lao She's novel *Rickshaw* (University of Hawaii Press, 1979) is a 1936 Chinese classic whose hero, 'Camel' Xiangzi, is a new arrival in Beijing from the countryside. He scrimps and saves to buy his own rickshaw, only to have it stolen when he ventures outside the city walls into the chaos gripping the countryside in the 1930s. From there it's strictly downhill, with each little step forward followed by two steps back. Jug Suraiya's *Rickshaw Ragtime: Calcutta Remembered* (Penguin Books, 1993) is a sympathetic account of life in Calcutta and, naturally, features rickshaws.

Rickshaws appear peripherally in many films but they play key roles in three very diverse movies. They're right at the center of Roland Joffé's 1992 *City of Joy*, a strictly one-dimensional film with larger-than-life heroes, led by Patrick Swayze as a disillusioned American doctor searching for enlightenment, and worse than bad villains, led by nasty Art Malik. The rickshaws roll in and out of scenes that will be familiar to any Calcutta visitor, including the idiosyncratic old Fairlawn Hotel. (Guests at the Fairlawn will find various reminders of the film crew's visit to the hotel.)

Even though Peter Weir's atmospheric 1983 film of *The Year of Living Dangerously* was actually filmed in the Philippines (what really happened in 1965 is still a sensitive subject in Indonesia), the settings are authentically tropical and the cycle-rickshaws which so regularly roll across the background are real Jakarta becaks. Mel Gibson and Sigourney Weaver star in the film, but it was Linda Hunt, playing the (male) dwarf news photographer Billy Kwan, who walked off with the Oscar.

After *The Scent of the Green Papaya*, Vietnamese director Hung Tran Anh turned his talents to the dark, depressing and confusing but certainly stylish *Cyclo* (1995). His vision of an amoral and violent Saigon won him no friends in government circles. In a story with remarkable similarities to Lao She's classic novel *Rickshaw* and Italian director Vittorio De Sica's equally classic 1947 film *The Bicycle Thief*, the 18-year-old cyclo rider has his cycle-rickshaw stolen and is drawn into a life of crime in order to repay his utterly ruthless female boss. To complicate matters further, the moody boss of his street gang is also a pimp for curiously perverted Saigon businessmen and the cyclo rider's older sister becomes one of his prostitutes.

Right
A rickshaw takes a young schoolboy past New Market in central Calcutta.

Us

We set out to create this book for a variety of reasons – partly to record a fascinating means of transport and human activity before it disappeared, partly because rickshaws are wonderfully varied examples of technical ingenuity, partly because they're often beautiful examples of folk art and partly because it looked like a fun thing to do. In fact the last part of that equation proved to be the biggest surprise of all. Putting this book together has been enormous fun and in very large part because of the people we've met – the rickshaw pullers and riders, the rickshaw owners and operators, the rickshaw makers and repairers. They've all had a tale to tell and they've all been remarkably enthusiastic about telling those tales.

As soon as we showed we were genuinely interested in their lives and their machines, we were welcomed into the rickshaw fraternity. In Calcutta we found ourselves sitting down with rickshaw pullers in their dormitories to hear about how much money they made and how much paperwork the state government inflicted upon them. In Yogyakarta we were proudly shown how brand-new becaks were made. In Penang riders revealed the important difference between a 20-tooth rear sprocket (easier cruising) and a 22-tooth sprocket (easier to pull away from a start), and warned about taking care if two fat customers climbed on or off at the same instant (they can tip the trishaw over). In Dhaka rickshaw artists showed us how they painted and decorated a new rickshaw. In Manila riders revealed how loading your sidecar with 100 lb of stereo equipment might make it harder work but certainly attracts more customers. Everywhere we were shown kindness, helpfulness and amazing interest. To all of you rickshaw people everywhere, a very big thank you.

To cover the 12 cities in this book we made three separate trips over a total of 45 days using 11 different airlines to make 26 flights. The temperatures varied from -1°C (30°F) in Beijing to +44°C (111°F) in Dhaka. Richard shot over 8000 frames of film while in each city Tony measured, weighed and tested the rickshaws. In nearly every city we started our rickshaw investigations by jumping in a rickshaw and asking the rider to 'show us the town'. In Singapore a rider, whom we will leave nameless, took us on a trishaw tour of the city's little known red light district, where prostitutes and their clients can 'go to their hiding place' if the authorities turn up on one of their occasional sweeps. Then, our rider reported, you can 'do your business behind locked doors' and, in efficient Singapore, 'satisfaction is guaranteed'. On the equivalent tour in Penang our slightly bemused rider pointed out the backpacker hostels where, he announced, 'Foreigners sleep all together, row by row.'

Left
In Agra rickshaw rider Saleem Khan handles the camera, Tony prepares to pedal off and Richard braces himself for the ride of his life.

Bottom (from left to right)
At a depot in Agra Tony discusses the rickshaw business.

Richard photographs Nino Quilon's full stereo sidecar in Manila.

An autorickshaw overtakes Tony as he test rides a rickshaw in the cantonment district of Agra. Moments later he mysteriously veered off the road.

In every city we weighed the rickshaws by the simple process of leveling the wheels and weighing each one in turn with a bathroom scale. Here Tony checks the weight of a Calcutta rickshaw.

Richard photographs a cyclo full of ducks in Hanoi.

Lounging back in a long and low Penang trishaw, Tony goes for a ride.

Locked out on the balcony of a Little India jewelry store, Richard waits for an evening trishaw tour to appear.

Index

Thanks

Thanks from Tony

Thanks to Alex Newton for his Dhaka advice and for tracking down a copy of *The Rickshaws of Bangladesh*. In Penang particular thanks to local historian Khoo Su Nin, whose book *Streets of George Town Penang* is a wonderful introduction to the architecture of her delightful city (trishaws roll through lots of the evocative pictures). Arthur R Kroeber's on-going history of Beijing provided some invaluable insights to the Beijing rickshaw story. We had expert assistance from translators in a number of cities and I'd particularly like to thank Fan Yue in Beijing, Hoang in Hanoi, Catalina Chan in Hong Kong, Arnold Legaspi in Manila and U Hla Min in Rangoon.

Many of the rickshaw people we met during our 12-city circuit appear in this book but there were an even greater number who are not credited. To all of them my sincere thanks. Richard was the ideal travel companion and I'd particularly like to thank him for not fighting over the Burmese reclining Buddha statue which I spotted only a micro-second before him in a Penang antiques shop and, on our inter-city flights, for letting me have the window seat more often than my fair share. I'll forget the occasion in Hanoi where the hotel receptionist suggested that, as the 'old man', I should have the downstairs room and the 'young man' could climb the extra flight of steps.

As usual my major thanks go to Maureen, who has ridden so many rickshaws with me in the past, and will again in the future.

. . . and from Richard

Assignments like this are special. It's been a great privilege and lots of fun to collaborate with Tony on such an ambitious project. I usually travel alone, so it was a revelation to find myself in the company of someone who walks as fast as me (which is how he got to the reclining Buddha first), and who is as keen to rise early for a *roti chanai* before the day's work begins.

I, too, sincerely thank all the rickshaw people who so willingly agreed to be watched, questioned and photographed while they went about their work.

Finally, a very special thank you to my wife, Iris, whose ability to juggle her life around mine is vital to our family's well-being, although she does think it's been too long since her last rickshaw ride.

...and from Lonely Planet

Chasing Rickshaws was edited at Lonely Planet's Melbourne office by Michelle de Kretser and Janet Austin. Simon Bracken designed the book, Geoff Stringer drew the technical illustrations with help from Simon and Paul Clifton, and the map was drawn by Rachael Scott. Annalisa Giudici, Graham Imeson and Vicki Beale helped pull it all together.

The photographs in this book are available from
Lonely Planet Images.
email: lpi@lonelyplanet.com.au

Australia
PO Box 617,
Hawthorn,
Victoria 3122
tel: (03) 9819 1877
fax: (03) 9819 6459
email: talk2us@lonelyplanet.com.au

USA
150 Linden St,
Oakland, CA 94607
tel: (510) 893 8555
TOLL FREE: 800 275-8555
fax: (510) 893 8563
email: info@lonelyplanet.com

www.lonelyplanet.com
AOL keyword: lp

UK
10a Spring Place,
London NW5 3BH
tel: (0171) 428 4800
fax: (0171) 428 4828
email: go@lonelyplanet.co.uk

France
71 bis rue du Cardinal-Lemoine,
75005 Paris
tel: 01 44 32 06 20
fax: 01 46 34 72 55
email: bip@lonelyplanet.fr
Minitel: 3615 lonelyplanet (1,29 F/mn)